Untold Stories

by an Old Storyteller

Untold Stories

by an Old Storyteller

George Gdovin

FB Fahrenheit Books

Guilford, CT

Fahrenheit Books

An imprint of OmicronWorld Entertainment LLC
42 Water Street, Suite 222 | Guilford, CT 06437
Visit our website at http://www.omicronworld.com

ISBN: 978-0-9968785-7-9 trade paperback via KDP

Date of Publication 15 January 2026

It is with deepest respect and gratitude that I dedicate this book to my three siblings.

They helped me to survive my growing years and are helping me enjoy my senior years.

My sister
Gloria
for her genuine love and caring.

My brother
Joseph
for being the older brother and resource person for many of my stories.

And for
my late younger brother
Bob
who, when I think of him,
always brings back memories of
our many adventures together.

CONTENTS

Publisher's Note

THE STORIES IN THIS BOOK ARE BASED ON REAL EVENTS. AS IN the author's companion title prior to this, *Memories, Memoirs & Miracles*, some poetic license has been taken by the author for purposes of clarity and cohesiveness of details.

Chapter 1
A Blue-Collar Introduction

Our old Wallingford homestead was one among many stark factory houses dotting all along the neighborhoods north of the railroad tracks. Each of the single and multifamily houses were separated from each other by driveways.

The neighbors comprised low- to moderate-income families. There were three very busy factories located well within walking distance of our front door. This arrangement was typical for our side of town. There were well defined asphalt or crushed stone driveways separating the single and multifamily houses along our block. The separations were compensated for by several front and side porches.

To the degree that the driveways isolated houses and families, the porches drew them back together. We all knew each other and shared the neighborhood.

Front porches were not only homey they also provided a focal point for families to gather and relax after working all day. In addition, many seniors would use their porches as a place to smoke a cigar or have a bowl of ice cream after supper. No one in our neighborhood had dinner, but we all had supper.

There were several races, colors, and nationalities integrated into our five blocks. Most of the adults worked all day in the surrounding factories and the kids went to the area public schools.

The old neighborhood generated very little ethnic discrimination, and if it was present, I wasn't aware of it. We all walked to school and most of the parents walked to work together. Maybe we were all too tired to bother with topics like discrimination. We all worked hard at full-time jobs in the area sweatshops or at part-time jobs after and before school. We were all just trying to get through the day with as little aggravation and as much comfort as possible.

Many of our early childhood friends were Puerto Rican. The Torres and the Santos families lived four and six houses down the block and grew up with us. Fast forward from the late 1950s to the early 1980s and we find our old neighborhood very integrated. Many of the kids we played ball with, in the lot near our house, we later played poker and drank beer with.

There were several small neighborhood bars throughout the town, all usually busy with the midday regulars and the night crowd. The local bars had the business advantage of having built-in crowds of customers. They changed with the local factory shift changes. Many of these neighborhood bars were bought by people living in the area.

There suddenly sprang up an Italian club, a Polish club, and a Spanish club, all on our side of town. Also, several public bars and restaurants emigrated from other neighborhoods. It was not unusual for these watering holes to share customers.

In the final analysis, Wallingford became known for its colorful clubs, bars, and restaurants. At one point their numbers were well into double digits, and many of them were within walking distance, of each other. When asked why Wallingford had so many food and liquor outlets, one bar owner replied, "Because the residents support us."

Then in 1978 two infamous café/bars emerged, one from the north and the other from the south sides of town. Both establishments had mixed crowds of people causing the local authorities to brand them potential powder kegs.

On the South side was the Monte Carlo Cafe, 80 percent Latino. It had pool tables, pinball machines, a jukebox, and a young to middle-aged clientele. The owner operator was a well-educated handsome young man named Gary.

On the north side was a similar spot named Fiddler's Green Cafe. The clientele was a very mixed crowd. They served good cafe style food and a varied assortment of bar drinks to accommodate the tastes of assorted patrons. The owners were two handsome, well-educated, young, streetwise brothers named Bob and George.

Both establishments were owned, operated, and supported primarily by local people and their sides of town, respectively. Both owners were Wallingford residents who grew up in those houses and went through school in town. They were not unfamiliar faces.

To the surprise of many, neither hangout, as they were referred to, had many incidents requiring police action. They both had rules that allowed patrons (male, female, other) to enjoy the eating, drinking, and sports in a relatively safe environment. All incidents were handled in-house by the owners, keeping in mind that they also agreed to share in reciprocal street law enforcement.

This hopefully provides an overview of an upper lower-class section of a middle-class town. It could also be interpreted as a typical blue-collar factory town in the state of Connecticut USA circa the early 1960s.

This is the socioeconomic setting for the short sketches that follow. The background information enables the reader to place the stories and characters in real time and space.

The sketches are based on true events involving real characters written by someone from inside the culture at the place and time.

Chapter 2
Circa November 1963
Brodi Picks a Winner

Our good friend Joe Brodi considered himself a professional horse race handicapper. He especially loved picking and betting horses at Roosevelt Raceway, in Westbury, New York. Roosevelt only ran trotters and almost exclusively at night.

Trotters are a horse pulling a two-wheeled cart called a sulky occupied by a single rider. They race around an oval track twice, typically in groups of eight. Our boy Brodi loved going to the trotters, especially at Roosevelt. He often spent hours each day reading the racing forms and horse racing newspapers. He usually did this study in Fiddler's Green Cafe or the Monte Carlo Cafe. Both safe places.

He had a special table near the front window of Fiddlers that everyone knew not to take. Brodi would be in promptly at 11 a.m.

Joe would order his lunch with an extra-large ginger ale soda. This would get him his small table as a customer and not as a loiterer. Plus, he was a very likable character, with the emphasis on the word character.

Joe would study the scratch sheets for hours and pick two or three horses for that night's races.

His short-necked friend, known as No Neck, usually hung out with Joe. He was also an easy person to be with, so long as you didn't offer him a job.

Brodi, would often tell the bar crowd what his picks were for that night. This made him an open target for laughter and joking.

Joe and No Neck would usually decide by mid-afternoon at what time they would head for the track and which horses they would bet.

The afternoon bar-guys would always ask Brody what his picks were and spend a while kidding him. A standing joke was, "Hey Brodi, did you bet your buddy's neck on your picks from last night?" That was always followed by a chorus of laughter.

It seemed that Joe and No Neck enjoyed the attention. Joe would make his announcement every day right about 3 p.m. just after No Neck arrived. Fiddler's Law only allowed regular customers to join in the daily roasting.

If George or Bob thought anyone was abusing the pair they would immediately be thrown out, which also meant no service at the Monte Carlo.

If on occasion the boys hit a winner, they always bought the afternoon crowd a round of drinks. This eventually became a ritual at Fiddler's.

One typical November day the boys made their 3 p.m. announcement followed by laughter. No Neck then made another announcement that their second pick was a house favorite named "Fiddle Faddle."

He agreed to place any bets the boys wanted, but only to win. Carefully going down the bar he collected an even $80 — with the slips to tell who bet and how much — and then the boys were on their way to New York.

When the two handicappers arrived at the track, No Neck knew of two items to attend to ASAP. One was to get all the bets in on Fiddle Faddle. The second was to get one of the boiled hot dogs with sauerkraut and yellow mustard. They were served at the bar on the grandstand level.

The boys were finally settling into their favorite seats, at the far end of the main level. They began to get comfortable. Joe had all his sheets to go over and a nice cold ginger ale to sip. No Neck had his hot dog with a large ginger ale, except his drink had two shots of whiskey tossed in. He claimed it was for his cold.

The first six races went off with no serious bets by the boys. They were patiently waiting for the 7th, the feature race. Joe suddenly noticed that Fiddle Faddle had been bumped up to the feature race. He was now going off at 27–1, up from 35-1 and now the fifth favorite.

Joe quickly assessed the situation and realized for Fiddle Faddle to be pushed up to the feature race and go off at 27-1, somebody had dumped a load of cash on him to win.

Joe turned to No Neck and told him their plan had changed. They were betting all their cash on Fiddle Faddle in the 7th to win.

No Neck, behind the two shots of whiskey, did not get overly excited and asked Brodi if he would like another ginger ale. He was going to get one for himself after making the bets.

The bets were in! No Neck got another ginger ale and met Brodi back at the end of the main concourse. That was their favorite area considering the bar, the restrooms and betting windows were all on the same level.

The crazy New York crowd seemed more restless and excited than usual about the upcoming feature race. Our boys had been at the track many times for as many feature races, but why all the fuss?

Then Joe saw on the front page of his program that this race was a very important last link to a new progressive bet offered exclusively at Roosevelt Raceway. The general idea was that winners had to be picked over more than one race and over more than one day. The payouts often ran into many thousands of dollars.

The final leg of the progressive bet would be the winner of today's feature race. It was rumored that there was a very large crowd holding numbers one and six. This meant they needed horse #1 or #6 to fill their cards. This also meant there would be a large pot of money to be divided by the winners.

The fact that #1 was the favorite to win followed by #6 as the third favorite only added to the tension. The large number of those lucky bidders still holding hot tickets had an excellent chance to cash in for big money.

The crowd slowly filled the main concourse to watch the race inside on the monitors. The screens were mounted overhead all along each level.

The fans anxiously waited for the race to begin. They spread from the outside grandstands up to the main bars along the second level. It was a very mild night so there were hundreds of fans outside. Then came the announcement, "The horses are approaching the gate, this can only mean one thing. It is now post time."

The air was thick with excitement and expectation. The outside racing fans also approached the rail at the finish line.

The tote board flashed the final odds and the amounts of money bet on each entry. Surprisingly, Fiddle Faddle ended up the fourth favorite with another large amount bet on him one minute before post time. The amount bet was enough to push Fiddle Faddle from 27-1 to 17-1. The more money bet, the lower the odds go.

A move like that indicated that someone didn't want the betting fans to follow the money and change the odds. This was accomplished by waiting at the betting window with a large amount of cash, then making the bet in the last minute before post-time. The New York fans did take notice, too late to do anything about it. The race was off!

The #1 horse went off at 2-1 while Fiddle Faddle ended up a 17-1 long shot. This was much to the delight of the person or persons who bet large amounts of cash on #1.

The horses reached the first turn with the #1 horse out in front. Fiddle Faddle—horse #8—was in the middle of the pack as they headed down the back stretch for the first time.

Fiddle Faddle was #5, maintained sixth position to the top of the back stretch. At this point, the order of positions was: #1, #6, #3, and #5. Suddenly, heading into the top of the far turn one horse cut directly in front of another causing the #3, the #2, and the #4 horses to lose control. This left only the #1, #5, #6, and #8 horses still in the race. The #1 horse, having been bumped, was forced to make a wide turn at the top of the stretch. The driver saved the day by taking the turn wide to avoid several crashes and horses that broke stride.

The #6 horse was ahead of the pack at the time of the pile ups, leaving a clean space between him and the traffic jam. Fiddle Faddle trailed well behind the pack allowing him to maneuver around the pile up and take third position. Finally, the #3 horse was in the mix of sulkies going into the turn and somehow survived but was slowed to almost a complete stop.

In the final turn at the top of this stretch the #6 and #1 horses were in front followed by Fiddle Faddle.

At the top of the stretch horses #6 and Fiddle Faddle were neck and neck. The favorite, #1, was expected to pull to the lead and win the race, but as they closed in on the finish line, Fiddle Faddle took the lead. The spectators went wild.

As the leaders were pressing in on the finish line #1 made a last effort. This push got him across the finish line ½-a-length ahead of #5 and two lengths ahead of #6. The fans were standing, shouting and cheering, the favorite had won!

About a minute or two after the race the word "official" was flashing on the tote board. Then an amazing second flash appeared announcing that an inquiry was called.

It is very unusual for an inquiry to be posted after the race was declared official. After the results were declared official it was not unusual for race fans to rip up or toss their tickets in the air in defeat. This resulted in the floor of the main concourse to be covered with hundreds of discarded tickets.

Less than one minute later a second surprise flashed on the board. It showed the word inquiry was being replaced with the word official again. Then came the third surprise. It showed the #1 horse being disqualified for fouling the #7 horse at the top of the fourth turn.

Then came the last surprise flash on the tote board — the #5 horse, Fiddle Faddle, was posted as the official winner paying $35.80 for first, $20.10 for place, and $8.60 to show.

Suddenly the crowd realized that the #1 horse was disqualified, which also cut the favorite out of the progressive bet pool. This was a significant loss for all those ticket holders. The fans were so enraged that they stormed out of the main concourse down to the grandstands and out onto the track.

Many of the mob were kicking the lights out of the tote board. Others pulled away pieces of the tote board fascia and proceeded to light them on fire.

While the mob was busy destroying the in-field array, Joe Brodi put his mind to work coming up with a brilliant idea, topping all his past schemes.

He grabbed No Neck and told him to take off his three-quarter-length coat, put it on the floor and run it to the opposite end of the concourse rounding up as many tickets and stubs as he could carry. In the meantime Joe was going to the car to wait for No Neck at the door of the ground floor exit.

Joe told No Neck to move as fast as he could. Joe knew it would only be a matter of minutes before the fans caught on to what he was up to.

No Neck asked Joe if he would have time to stop and cash in a few winning tickets and grab a quick hot dog? Joe shook his head and replied, "You dumb-ass, if the fans who lost their tickets catch you, you'll be in the same shape as the tote board." No Neck heard the message loud and clear.

Joe had the car at the exit and No Neck, who was very fleet of foot, raced to the car and jumped in to make their getaway.

Meanwhile, the whole track complex was swarming with cops and security. The fire department had trucks and hoses stretched anywhere they could run them to the infield. This served as a perfect cover for our hometown gang heading back to Fiddler's.

Just outside the track area Joe pulled into a rest stop to take a quick break and start counting out their newly acquired treasurer. They readily found several win tickets at $35.80, a good number of place tickets at $20.10, and a few show tickets at $8.60.

After a short rest Joe decided to go back to the track after everything had calmed down. Joe wanted to cash in the original $80 bets from Fiddlers and a few hundred dollars for him and No Neck.

Joe had no problem repeating to No Neck that it was his idea to have all their bankroll bet on Fiddle Faddle, following the sudden drop in odds.

Having cashed in several hundreds of dollars of No Neck's original bets and $400 or $500 of their newly acquired stash, they, once again, were ready to go home.

The next day when the afternoon crowd showed up at Fiddler's, no neck handed out over $1400 in cash. No Neck was a hero in every sense of the word.

The winners proceeded to cheer and buy several rounds of drinks. The money stayed in the neighborhood.

The afternoon and night crowds both asked the same question. "How could Brodi have ever picked a 17-1 winner like Fiddle Faddle?"

Joe slowly turned toward the bar and, with a serious face, explained, "When you learn how to handicap like No Neck and myself, studying the programs, the various scratch sheets and even the weather, you qualify for entry into the handicapping big leagues. But first it takes hours of analysis analyzing all the facts and statistics, it is obviously a learned discipline."

Following that detailed answer to the afternoon crowd, Joe turned back toward the bar with a smug look and said, "Mr. No Neck and I will be leaving shortly for the Monte Carlo Cafe to visit my dear friend Gary and make a little splash in the old neighborhood." Joe then said in a very sincere voice, "We're keeping it local, boys."

Chapter 3

The Lost Wedding Ring

So, how do you lose a bride's gold wedding ring in front of 150 people during a wedding ceremony? This question seemed to be echoing throughout the old Grange Hall.

It was my nephew Peter's wedding. He had studied for the priesthood for several years until he met his wife-to-be, Diana. They were a very reserved couple.

Cousin Angelo was their best man and had both rings in his pocket. He was also the person responsible for organizing the reception. Earlier in the day, he had set up a display of fresh flowers and wedding presents on a small table in front of the head table. This was where Father Sullivan would perform the ceremony.

Everyone found their seats and were waiting for the ceremony to begin.

Included in this crew were several Italian cousins, aunts, and uncles who had driven from Brooklyn, New York, along with their children. Aunt Helen was known for making the best sauce in the family. She was the outgoing type. She also thought she was a good opera singer, especially following a few glasses of wine.

Uncle Louis, a semi-retired union mason, was there. He was wearing his black suit and white tie with his union pin tie tack. His son Tommy was at the same table with his wife, Angie, and their two young boys. They were both good parents. But the whole family was aware that Angie had a tendency to be a little over-protective of the two boys, while Tommy was the complete opposite.

A small band was setting up in a corner of the hall. They consisted of a guitar, accordion, drummer, and a young woman singer. The name of the group was Stanley and the Truetones. Unfortunately, Stanley died three years prior and was replaced by Jeff, who was also a guitarist. They never changed the name of the band because they didn't want to have new cards printed. Peter the drummer had "Stanley" painted in gold on his bass drum. It was a low-budget production.

The tables were almost all filled, and they looked nice with white tablecloths and a vase of artificial flowers on each.

The open bar had been serving soft drinks and Uncle Joe's homemade wine, along with beer and hard liquor. Uncle Joe claimed he was catering to the early arrivals, although serving drinks before the meal was not recommended.

My great Uncle Chicky was an early arriver. He had been a used car salesman most of his life and eventually owned two large car sales and service dealerships somewhere in New Jersey. He was old now and confined to a wheelchair. His custom chair was equipped with a small electric motor, a built-in ashtray, and a cup holder. He claimed the banquet table closet to the bar.

My 50-year-old cousin Helena was a very Christian woman all her adult life. She worked as an aide of some sort at a cloistered Dominican Convent a few towns over. Whenever she got excited or frightened, she would whip out her rosary beads and start praying out loud. I didn't suppose there was anything wrong with praying.

When the wedding ceremony was only moments from beginning, the bar was slowly closing. Cousin Angelo was the last to leave the bar. He was a feisty fellow, and kind of small in stature. He and Cousin Ben sampled the wine to be sure it was just right for the toast later.

It was approaching 3 p.m. and the time for the ceremony. Everyone was excited and there was lots of chatter. The hall was alive with anticipation. Even Cousin Claire, who was legally deaf, said she felt the excitement in the air.

The wedding party and Father Sullivan slowly approached the small table, with the real flowers, to get started. The guests finally quieted down.

As the wedding party gathered around the table, the bride and groom chatted with Father Sullivan. He quickly reviewed the simple steps leading up to putting the rings on the bride and groom, to be followed by his blessing.

Father asked Cousin Angelo if he had the rings. The bride's wedding band had a small diamond, and the groom's ring was a traditional gold band. Angelo apparently didn't hear him. At this point everyone was in a festive mood. It was plain to see that the bar had been well-visited prior to the beginning of the ceremony.

Father Sullivan asked Angelo to stand next to the groom and for the maid of honor to stand next to the bride. It was a very intimate and orderly start to a life-long commitment.

Father Sullivan asked Cousin Angelo a second time if he had the rings, Angelo, who had spent a considerable amount of time testing the temperature of the wine with Uncle Joe and Uncle Chicky, snapped back, "Of course I do. Do you think I ran off with them?" With that, Angelo grabbed open his suit jacket and in one swoop, snatched the two rings from the inside lapel pocket.

It was the theatrics of Angelo's attempt to deliver the rings into Father Sullivan's hand that caused a series of uniquely bizarre events to unfold.

Between his exaggerated motion to open his jacket and the amount of wine he consumed earlier Angelo lost his balance. In an almost dance-like attempt to steady himself and hand the two rings to the Father's hand, both rings flew into the air and bounced off a large flowerpot on the table.

The groom's ring dropped to the floor, as Diana's ring was in the liftoff stage of an incredible journey.

The groom's ring hit the bright green foil wrap on the pot, but Diana's ring ricocheted off the ceramic pot like a bullet.

The concerned crowd yelled, "No Angelo!!" as Father Sullivan and he both lunged forward to intercept the rings in flight.

Unfortunately, they were both headed for the small table. The left front leg of the table collapsed under Father Sullivan's weight, which sent the plants and potting soil in all directions. Much of the soil landed on the bride's and groom's shoes.

Angelo, being lighter in weight than the good Father, glanced off the edge of the collapsing table onto the hardwood floor with a clap.

Since the rings were circular, they could, under the right conditions, take on all the characteristics of small wheels.

Well, the perfect storm was about to take place. Diana's ring hit the floor and spun and rolled directly toward the bar. The ring hit the base of the bar and found its way — as though under demonic guidance — directly into the small hot air vent next to the beer cooler.

As the wedding party began chasing the rings, the seated guests became uneasy and a bit vocal. It began with loud whispers that quickly got louder. Since Cousin Claire was legally deaf, she unknowingly shouted, "Who is the dumb ass who lost the rings!?" thinking she was speaking at a normal level.

Uncle Joe, having never left his spot at the bar, sprang off his stool in a fruitless attempt to save the day.

He missed the ring but slid headfirst to the edge of the air vent.

Angelo took out his pocketknife and proceeded to pry the metal vent out of the floor. He immediately began to reach down into the ductwork, trying to reclaim the ring.

Uncle Joe assisted with a flashlight. As he nudged Angelo aside, a comment was made referring to the length of Angelo's stubby arms.

Uncle Joe took the job over and let Angelo hold the flashlight. They argued for a bit regarding whose arms were longer, then they both agreed to take a wine break.

In the meantime, Father Sullivan assured the guests they would soon have both rings, and the ceremony would go on. A few of the family members from Brooklyn asked if the bar was going to reopen. Father Sullivan was all for it, but the bride did not agree. "No more booze until after the meal," she announced. "I don't want this to turn into any more of a circus than it already is!"

The boys at the air vent adjourned to the bar. They needed a new way to get to the ring. Knowing that the coal-fired furnace was not in use and had been taken apart for cleaning, a new plan was born.

They all agreed that Angelo would reach into the furnace in the cellar and see if the ring had made it that far. They also voted to move their base of operation to the furnace room.

Uncle Louis thought that since he was a mason, he knew how the old furnaces were built. He grabbed a bottle of wine and joined forces with the ad hoc work crew.

When they reached the furnace room, they quickly realized that the top of the fire chamber had been removed from the ancient furnace. All the ductwork that led directly to the plenum above the furnace, and pieces of the plenum had been removed for repair and cleaning.

They all now knew that the ring could have rolled all the way down the air duct into the fire chamber. With this awareness, the new plan was to open the large furnace door and let Angelo reach inside, headfirst, to hopefully retrieve the ring. Angelo was the smallest and would fit through the large cast iron door accessing the chamber.

Angelo was ready. In he went headfirst through the furnace doorway. He was up to his waist when he yelled, "I found the f%&#-ing ring!" It seemed too good to be true. The guests upstairs probably heard Angelo yell. His loud voice echoed throughout the entire duct system, and, unfortunately, through the floor vents of the upstairs hall.

Adding to the chaos, when Angelo attempted to back out of the furnace, his belt and pants caught on some part of the cast iron door inside the chamber.

The team pulled on both of his legs, trying to get him free. At this point in the operation, Angelo started to holler and swear in a billowing voice. His desperate voice broadcast clear as a bell from each of the floor vents. He blasted out the most vicious litany of curses and swearing phrases known in both the English and Italian languages.

When we ran back upstairs to check on the guests, we found a scene from a typical Marx Brothers movie or Three Stooges show – and saw the appalled looks on many faces, while others laughed uproariously. Angelo's voice blasted in curses, addressing everyone on the planet, including several references to the Pope!

Angie ran around the table trying to cover her boy's ears, while one of the aunts from Brooklyn ran between the tables praying in Italian and showering all those around her with Holy Water. She always carried Holy Water in her purse, for just such events that needed cleansing.

At the same time, Aunt Helen, also from Brooklyn, got very upset and, as usual, started singing a scene from Pagliacci. She was doing okay until she tried going down on one knee to imitate Enrico Caruso at the Met. She had had a few wines, which helped her to lose her balance. Her nephew helped her up and she decided to join the ladies at the next table, saying the rosary out loud. They hoped to drown out Angelo's recital of curses, but it didn't work.

Meanwhile, Father Sullivan was pacing through the tables trying to reassure the guests that all was going to be fine.

The bride and groom were upset, to say the least, and said in unison, "The hell with it! Open the bar and start up the band!" This diversion tactic was successful. The Truetones effectively drowned out Angelo.

The circus was surely in full, three-ring mode. Even Uncle Chickey somehow managed to sample enough of Uncle Joe's homemade wine to fall asleep in his wheelchair. One of Tommy's kids accidentally bumped the wheelchair as both boys ran between the tables to keep away from their mom. The bump to the wheelchair was not enough to rouse Chicky. However, it did cause him to slowly slide off the chair onto the floor.

The boys thought Chicky was dead and began yelling, "Uncle Chicky is dead!" This caused a major stir. Some of the older women made signs of the cross and prayed out loud for him.

Then as suddenly as the fiasco had begun it stopped.

Out from the cellar door came the ring rescue crew. Angelo was covered with soot and his pants were ripped open at the front buckle. But he was most decidedly the hero of the day.

The disheveled crowd sang out in a unified cheer, and even Uncle Chicky came back to life and joined in the celebration, while sitting on the floor.

The bride and groom made it known that they still wanted to finish the ceremony. They cleaned up Angelo and pinned his pants closed in case he wanted to dance later. They requested the wedding party to regroup.

Father Sullivan came from the bar and announced he was going to perform an edited version of the ceremony, stating, "We men of the cloth must learn to adapt to any manner of adverse conditions."

He had the rings and now the shortened ceremony and vows could be completed. The ceremony lasted all of five minutes. Uncle Louie said, "All I heard was 'I now pronounce you man and wife.'"

The band began to play, the chicken and pasta dinner went well, and after cleaning the potting soil off the dance floor, the beautiful bride and handsome groom danced the first dance.

Chapter 4

The Train Robbers

Around 7 a.m. on a Wednesday the early edition of the local paper hit the stands. The headline in bold type read, "Train Robbers Strike Again."

The headline led readers to believe another train had been robbed. A more accurate headline would have read, "Robbers from Train Strike Again."

A not-so-simple explanation would be that during the mid-1950s to late-1960s there were a number of armed robberies executed by passengers from the daily commuter trains. The trains involved ran between New York and Boston. They stopped at most larger cities along the way, one stop in the morning, and again in late afternoon.

Taking into consideration the many stops, it was duly nicknamed, "The Milk Run." For the convenience of its commuters, some of the stops were as long as 40 minutes. It was during one of these longer stops that our story begins.

During the morning stop in Wallingford, CT a brazen trio of armed robbers calmly exited the train. They rode in three different cars and spaced their offloading apart, to avoid being identified as a team. After leaving the train, they slowly regrouped on the small town green adjacent to the depot. From there they reviewed the plan. They decided which of the several bars, restaurants, or stores in the area appeared to be most vulnerable and most profitable. The target needed to be in close proximity to the depot for timing reasons.

Their basic plan was always the same. They would charge into one of the establishments they had previously cased, wearing ski masks, with guns drawn, swearing and shouting threats.

Having visited the chosen bar or store beforehand resulted in a few less surprises on robbery day. Experience taught them that one-room bars worked best. It always made crowd control more manageable, and bars had proven to be more profitable.

Making their grand entrance, flashing guns, and shouting, they quickly gained complete control of the patrons and employees. In extreme cases they would fire a random warning shot to be sure they had everyone's undivided attention.

The final preparatory step was to place a "Closed until tomorrow for repairs" sign on the front and back doors.

At this point the actual robbing would begin with emptying the register and frisking the patrons and employees for cash and jewelry. Following the personal shakedowns, the victims would be herded into the bathrooms. The doors were tied off from the outside, keeping everybody temporarily out of the way.

They found that by packing all the loot into their businessmen's briefcases they fit in with the flow of the commuter traffic without notice.

Their standard method of operation proved to be foolproof and very profitable for several years—until they made the mistake in mid-July 1971 to rob the American Grill.

This moderately sized bar and grill was on a busy highway close to the train depot, and thus very vulnerable.

Following their preparatory meeting the three robbers—Joe the boss, Carlos and Sam—headed around the corner toward the bar. All had gone thus far according to plan.

Unbeknownst to them they chose one of the most notorious bars in the area. It was a unique establishment with two large round windows in the front, and the front door equal distance between them. A sort of art deco style.

The bar was known in town as being a kind of retirement home for street survivors. It seemed to draw all the area retired con men, gamblers, hustlers, second-story men, card sharks, and a few bookies. As Momo often said, "And we even went so low as to allow a few politicians into visit only." Momo was the owner bartender and part time cook. It was not terribly difficult for Momo to multitask as cook and bartender when there were only eight to 10 customers at a time. They hung out in his bar every day regardless of the limited customer service.

Momo claimed he once owned a very exclusive restaurant at the shore. He claimed it was too much for him to run so he decided to downsize. Everyone knows he lost the restaurant and half his bankroll shooting craps and betting slow horses.

Just in case a crowd showed up he had a part-time cook who helped in the kitchen. His name was Dick Hadley. His full-time profession was scam artist. Dick's street name was Leonardo, as in Leonardo da Vinci. He was master at the art of the con.

Word had it that in his prime he made the who's who of high-end cons. It was true that one of his finer masterpieces was the sale of a fake Picasso painting to a non-English speaking lieutenant in the Chinese mafia.

Leo moved out of New York City very shortly after he got paid. He claims the cash was his retirement nest egg and he was getting tired of the city life.

Getting back to our train robbers, Sam, one of the gang members, mentioned several times to Joe and Carlos that the place gave him the creeps. He said the windows looked like 2 voodoo eyes staring right through him.

They told Sam to shut up and concentrate on the mission. Joe added, "This is just another building with a long bar and a few booths for seating. In fact, this joint is no different than the other bars we've robbed a few months ago."

Joe did pretty good in his description until he got to the part about the patrons. The American grill owner, patrons, and staff were not like all bars, as they were soon to find out. In fact, they might not have been like any bar near or far.

They waited a few minutes outside to be sure there was nobody entering or leaving. It was time, so they quickly pulled down their ski masks, checked their weapons, and we're ready to make their grand entry.

On the count of three they crashed through the door waving guns and shouting, "Everyone stay right where you are, and nobody will get hurt!"

Joe, who was the brains of the outfit, ordered everyone to put both hands on the bar and keep them there. This way Carlos and Sam could plainly see if anyone decided to be a hero.

Joe suddenly realized that all the shouting, swearing, and threatening didn't seem to be working on this crowd as quickly as usual. In fact, to Joe's surprise, only two of the six men at the bar even turned around to acknowledge their presence, and that was only to see what all the ruckus was about.

Momo shouted back, "If you cheap excuses for bandits don't calm down, we will throw your sorry asses out on the sidewalk, and all your toys along with you." Joe yelled an answer, "This is for real. We are really robbing this dump!"

At this point the boys at the bar began to get restless.

Baha Benny turned on his bar stool and advised the would-be robbers that their only option was to make a run for it while they still could. Joe returned the comment, "You good fellows seem to forget that we have the guns. In fact, do you see Sam standing there? His only job is to stand guard over the crowd and to shoot the first one of you bastards who gets too frisky."

Baha Benny, who took on all the characteristics of a gnarly old tree stump with an enlarged Mexican bandito head bolted on top, shouted, "If you know what's good for you, you and your friends should stop whatever it is that you are trying to do and leave quietly. Minnow needs quiet when picking his horse bets for the day. You're messing with the wrong crowd." Baha repeated the message in Spanish for Carlos.

Momo shouted to Joe, "Think about it, Einstein, what kind of people won't even turn around to see who's wearing ski masks, waving guns around at their heads?" Joe looked a little confused.

Baha, in the meantime, began staring down Carlos and Sam. He had machine gun eyes that could stare a rattlesnake into retreat and probably had. The machine gun eyes were definitely getting the boys nervous, especially Carlos.

The crowd, Cochise, and Eddie Z were still seated at the bar. Cochise was a Native American from upstate New York who ran his own small business. He ran homemade moonshine to two reservations up north once a week. His Native American brothers and sisters along with a few small liquor stores kept him in business for years. As Cochise often said, "If you have a good, dependable product, the world will beat a path to your teepee."

It was plain to see that he and the Kraut, a survivor of the Berlin Wall in Germany, were very easy to rile, especially when there were guns being waved around.

In a flash, Cochise pulled out a knife and had it at Carlos's throat before anybody could blink. Carlos in turn began a pathetic cry to spare his life.

Eddie Z saw it was time and flew off his stool, head butting and tackling Sam. He hit him so hard it caused Sam's pretty pearl-handled pistol to fly out of his hands high in the air.

Unfortunately, the steel barrel of the gun smashed a bottle of high-end vodka. To make matters worse the vodka drenched Momo, who was still behind the bar.

They say that in his day Eddie was an excellent bill collector for four or five of the local bookies. He was also known to have the hardest head around. Rumor had it that he could head-butt people and knock them unconscious.

At this juncture we had Sam on the floor in a headlock by Eddie. We also had Baja casually sitting on the barstool holding a double-edged boot knife to

Carlos's throat. Carlos was on the next stool, still begging for his life.

Joe was the only one of the robbers still standing, but not for long. As he stood facing the fiasco with his trusty pistol aimed at them all, he said in a deep scary voice, "The next man that moves will catch a bullet." To verify his threat, he turned and shot a round into the closest barstool. Momo immediately began cursing him and his family in Italian.

With that the Kraut made a move. Joe began to see what was unfolding and squeezed off another round into another stool hoping to scare him. This old standby tactic failed again, for the Kraut didn't scare easily, especially behind two or three shots of tequila for breakfast.

While the Kraut had Joe's attention, nobody noticed Leo quietly coming out of the kitchen. He approached Joe from behind and knocked him down while the Kraut grabbed his gun.

Leo advised Sam and Carlos to empty their pockets on the bar. Joe had the vodka-soaked pistol aimed at his head by vodka-soaked Momo. Minnow quickly grabbed the money on the bar and urged Momo and Cochise to shoot the three of them, then called the cops to see if there was a reward for their capture.

"Let's shoot them to end a crime wave and get the reward. It's a win-win deal for everybody."

Of course, there was no way for any of our train robbers to know that this wouldn't happen for two very good reasons. The primary reason was that they were not cold-blooded murderers and, second, if the cops did show up there was a very good chance the home team might end up in jail with Joe and the boys.

Eddie cringed when the word jail was used. He was still on probation for public drunkenness and destroying private property.

It was common street knowledge that he occasionally got very drunk and would run forward like a Raging Bull and slam into car doors. The damage could be extensive.

He managed to get away with it until he slammed into the mayor's wife's car. She was parked in front of Holy Trinity Church for bingo night.

In the course of 30 minutes the American grill went from being held hostage at gunpoint by three train robbers to a complete reversal of roles.

Carlos was still being held at knife point by Cochise.

Sam was being held at gunpoint with his own gun lost in the head-butt incident with Eddie. Sam was moaning about two probably broken ribs and Carlos just continued to plead for his life.

Our team now had all the guns, their money, personal ID, credit cards, 1 gold watch, a silver lighter, a little black book containing private material, and two rings not yet appraised.

The new dilemma was what to do with three previously armed robbers.

Then Leonardo came up with a plan. Like most of his plans they were a bit outside of the box, but that is why he was so respected.

His plan was, as he put it, "A win-win for the hometown favorites."

Purposely speaking loud enough for all to hear, Leo in a very matter-of-fact tone said, "It is a piece of cake. Part one, we shoot all three and pile them into the back of Kraut's pickup truck."

He went on, "Part two, Kraut and Eddie bring them to our town landfill. We pay our old drinking buddy Danny three times the usual amount and a $100 tip to make sure they disappear permanently."

Joe suddenly jumped in, "Listen, we can work this thing out with no messy shooting or hiding evidence. We will pay you $1000 each to let us go and never see or hear from us again."

The all-American team consulted and agreed to $5,000 cash. Leo went on to say, "This buys your way out. We will write down your phone numbers and addresses just in case we get lonely."

Then from behind the bar Momo added $400 for the two new bar stools and $50 for the broken vodka bottle.

All agreed but still were under the watch of kraut and Cochise. They were probably thinking about shooting somebody or something.

Leo then went on to explain that Joe would be traded for $5,450 by 10am tomorrow.

With that Carlos and Sam promised to get the money back by later that day. Carlos claimed to have contacts in New Haven.

Joe asked, "What about me while they are gone?" Momo looked at Leo indirectly, requested a quick consultation. The executive decision was that Joe be detained in the old-abandoned liquor closet/meat locker.

Joe then gave Sam another money contact in New Haven, just in case. He asked about using the men's room before getting locked up, and could they please leave the light on in his temporary quarters. Momo agreed and escorted Joe to the men's room with his own gun trained on him.

Momo patted down Joe as he returned from the men's room. Joe asked, "So, what do you think I am going to attack you with a roll of paper towels or maybe a soap dispenser?"

Momo replied, "Joe, can you see now why I am leading you around with your own gun? Joe, your professional demeanor stinks."

As he led Joe to his new quarters, Minnow handed Joe his newspaper and said, "This is in case you get bored in there. You will have a light on."

Leo warned the robbers, once again, that Momo had all their names, addresses, credit cards and licenses. The belongings will be returned when $5,450 was put on the bar.

All agreed and off went Sam and Carlos, with no hesitation. Joe was off to the old meat locker feeling better after realizing he was lucky Danny at the dump wasn't his escort. Momo handed Joe a bar stool to sit on. Momo added, "Joe please excuse the bullet hole. Rowdy customers."

Fast forward four hours. Back came the two robbers. They had a bag full of cash, two gold neck chains, and a Rolex watch.

Minnow patted them down and escorted them to a booth. Minnow said with a smirk on his face, "You good old boys obviously didn't visit your ATM to get that much cash and jewelry."

Sam said, "They just happened to stop at a private club for directions, and what do you know, an all-day and all-night crap and poker game was going on."

Since they already had their ski masks and a toy pistol they decided to jump the next train north. It worked!

"Of course," Sam stuttered out, "we will never show our faces in the New Haven area ever again. As we were safely leaving New Haven on the shuttle, we couldn't help but notice the boys from the club searching alleys and cars for us."

With all that said the crowd let Joe out of his confinement. He asked Minnow if he could take the paper with him. He wasn't finished reading it.

Momo urged that they get out of the bar soon, he noticed a couple of incoming customers. They agreed and asked if they could have a few beers to go.

In a parting gesture, Cochise handed Carlos back the silver inscribed lighter. He had noticed it was a birthday gift from the inscription.

In parting, Leo said to Joe, "Don't look at the money as ransom. Look at it as a storage fee."

Leo then reached in the money bag and handed them $50 each and told them, "If you hurry you can catch the 4:30 train to Grand Central."

Chapter 5
Chocolate Milk Resentment

Her name was Miss Haggerty, and she was my third-grade teacher. Her nickname of "Old Horseface," fit her perfectly. As Washington Irving wrote so eloquently, "The names Plowface or Horseface were not inapplicable to her person."

Third-grade kids can fit very descriptive names to anyone they target. Often such names are considered cruel, and yet often very fitting and accurate descriptions. The school janitor, Mr. Costello, received a debilitating injury to his right leg in World War II and walked with a heavy limp. I remember the kid saying, "Old peg leg is cleaning the corridor in front of room number six. He will chat with Horseface for a while, so it's safe to sneak a smoke."

The small janitor's room off the corridor had a strong exhaust fan built into the ceiling. The room had an area for the janitor to eat lunch and read the paper. The fan was installed to exit any smells from the cleaning supplies stored in the room, as well as the smoke from his regular a.m. and p.m. smoke breaks. But it was also the perfect clandestine place to sneak a smoke with the older guys so long as you had a good lookout.

When I first arrived in Wallingford from the Cheshire school system, I was enrolled in Washington Street School, which was already in the third week of the new school year. Miss Haggerty's seating plan was simple — six rows of desks facing a long slate chalkboard at the front of the room. Each row represented the scholastic standing of each student. Facing the class, the pupils highest in scholastic ability were the rows on the left. The lower achievers were in the rows along the windows on the far right side of the room.

Miss Haggerty had no problem discussing the scholastic significance of the rows or the pupils seated therein. As a newcomer, the way the kids explained it to me was, "The smarter kids were in rows one to four, and the dumbass kids were in rows five and six." I was assigned to the first seat in row six. This was not at all good for my self-esteem.

Setting aside the hierarchy of students by location, two additional downsides to being assigned row six were the glaring heat from the windows on a warm sunny day and cold drafts from the old windows when it was cold.

Every Monday, Wednesday, and Friday we had a class formally titled Basic Handwriting Skills. I dreaded Sunday nights in anticipation of the upcoming Monday morning's "Trial in India, Ink" as it was nick-named.

The gauntlet started with the passing out of very porous writing paper. Miss H. always chose someone from rows one or two to do that job. Secondly, the India ink bottles would be handed out and placed in each inkwell. The inkwell holders were built into the upper right corner of the desk. This job was, obviously, a highly skilled position considering the need for neatness in the task. The glorified job was awarded monthly to some academically deserving student — always chosen from rows one and two. Since there were six students in each row, the ink distribution task was a limited-access job opportunity.

Once the paper and ink were passed out, Miss H. would write the lesson on the chalkboard. The primary objective of the lesson was usually to copy a simple sentence in cursive handwriting.

Each student had an assigned wooden pen that held a simple metal pen point. The trick was to dip the metal pen point into the small bottle of the India ink and make it to the paper without losing any ink in flight. There were a limited number of spots any stray ink could land. One was the desktop, another was the paper, and the third was on the sleeve or hands of the writer. Precision was required and the process could make a student break out in a sweat.

Once the nib of the pen point was full of ink and safely transported to the paper, we could begin the writing assignment.

For us row sixers, it was important that we arrange the paper strategically over the hollow cracks in the desktop. The grooves and cracks were not in the wood desktop but in its layers of shellac. The desk surfaces had baked and cracked over so many years.

If you were at all heavy-handed with your pen, it would penetrate the paper and deliver the ink into the groove beneath. Unfortunately, the back side of the paper would quickly absorb the ink, making a perfect Rorschach inkblot. When this happened, we used to say, "You are a dead duck!"

About halfway through the morning, Old Horseface would declare a milk break. It was a degrading and embarrassing process for students from low-income families. We were all on a master list to determine who could and who would not have a free six-ounce bottle of milk, chocolate milk not included.

The usual list included Charlie T., Kenny H., Maria D., and me. We were consistently the four charity cases from row six.

After everyone from rows one through four got their milk, which included chocolate, Ms. H. would call us up one at a time by name. She was also sure to mention in a sing-song voice, "Remember, no chocolate milk for the free milk people."

I felt completely embarrassed and ashamed. If I didn't want the regular milk so badly, I would have said, "No thanks" but what I really wanted to say was, "Take your milks. Miss H. and shove them all including the chocolate milk!"

I was never sure how Maria, Kenny, and Charlie felt, but later learned that people show their embarrassment in a variety of ways. For instance, Charlie would immediately chug down the milk and slap the small round cardboard milk cap to his forehead. Because the cap was still wet with milk, it would stick. He would then turn toward rows one through five and make crazy faces for them. He reminded me of a court jester. Because Maria couldn't speak or understand English, she would smile and laugh with the other students. Kenny, however, was very solemn. I believe we had something in common. Following Charlie's sideshow, Miss. H. would announce, "Five more minutes to finish snacks." Then she would have a little pot of tea brewing and pour a bit of honey in it. She would sip it well after the snack period. I did notice that she smiled more often following her tea break.

Jimmy, from row three, told me, "No one had ever tasted, or seen, what she had in that honey bottle!" Pamela from row one claimed to have seen the small bottle. She said, "It looked like a bottle of snake oil or magic elixir I saw being sold by a traveling salesman in an old cowboy movie," No one really knew!

Unfortunately, what I did know was what discrimination felt like. I was also aware how powerful low self-esteem combined with discrimination could be. These elementary school experiences laid the foundation for many deep-seated and lasting resentments. Many of those unidentified resentments followed me well into my late 20s and early 30s.

It was due to my later education, work with health professionals, 12-step programs, and the aid of a spiritual adviser that I finally began to accept the reality of how much that third grade episode had impacted my life.

My elementary school experience can be viewed as a double-edged sword. On one hand, it helped me to better understand the pain of those trapped in discriminating environments, and on the other hand, it helped me to recognize discrimination in my own environment.

Finally, hindsight being 20-20, I needed to look back and understand that Miss Haggerty was probably never aware that discrimination and infectious hate ever existed in her classroom. For my own well-being, I needed to silently forgive her for her shortcomings and thank her for teaching me to write.

Chapter 6

Harry and the Cannon

Wanted, printers devil. High school student with Connecticut driver's license. Must be mechanically Inclined. Verification of minimum C average required. This was the job description I saw one day in high school.

"The printers devil will help the printers: 1) to monitor the lead melting crucible, 2) to meltdown lead ingots to supply linotype machines, 3) to help printers with page layout, 4) to help maintain all printer shop equipment, 5) help maintain a safe workplace for all employees, 6) Starting pay will be minimum wage."

When I saw the want ads on the student lobby bulletin board, I knew I had to apply.

I am sure part of my enthusiasm stemmed from my childhood neighbor Mr. Murray. He had retired many years before from a national newspaper. He loved telling us stories of his adventures working for the newspaper during World War II. He made the job sound exciting and adventurous.

Looking back, I believe my secondary reason might have been to find out what exactly a printer's devil does.

I was told there were several other students who were going to apply. They told me that they heard that printer's devils have a direct relationship with people, places, and things related to the "Dark Side."

I was told later that they all lost interest in the job and withdrew their applications following their first interview. They felt strongly about being expected to perform moderate amounts of manual labor, and that no phase of the job was affiliated with witchcraft or demonology. I also got the hint that some printer—a biker named Harty—was much too crude for their liking.

That narrowed the number of applicants to two other seniors. They were in the high school college preparation program and admitted that they were not too crazy with the term physical labor. Their visuals included more about writing and editing, and also, much less of Harry. The next day I called the print shop and asked where and when I should leave off my one paragraph resume and my B minus grade average. I was surprised and pleased to find the print shop to be our local newspaper. I like the sound of "I work part time for our local newspaper."

When I called the contact phone number, I was introduced to Maya the owner's wife who also functioned as the HR person. She got right to the point by asking, "George, if all your paperwork is in order and you are chosen to work here, when can you start?" I told her I could start the day I was hired. She liked that answer.

About four days went by until I got a call from Mr. K, the owner. His message for me was to report to the main office and get my paperwork done. Also, I should bring my driver's license. I was hired!

I was both happily surprised and anxious. This was my first real job, and I wanted things to go well. I couldn't wait to tell my family and friends.

I got off school early the next day to be sure I would have my paperwork in order. I had the feeling Mrs. K might be at the office waiting for me. She seemed like the anxious type.

Sure enough, there was Mrs. K with a stack of forms to fill out. I filled out the forms and gave them to her in her. She then told me she would put in a good word for me, followed by my first assignment, which was to sweep the office floor. I took it that this must be part of the interview process to weed candidates out.

The newspaper business was not all it was cracked up to be. I thoroughly considered quitting during my first 15 minutes on the job but that would classify me the same as the other applicants. Besides, Mrs. K asked me in a very polite way to sweep up the office.

It was about 30 minutes into my new job and successfully completed my first assignment. Clean floors!

About the same time Mr. K came walking in. He asked me to meet him in his office after I put the broom away.

I promptly put away the broom and met him in his private office. He welcomed me aboard and asked me to sit down. Having worked part-time jobs during my summer vacations, I knew getting called into the chief's office just 35 minutes into any new job was a bit unsettling. Although, considering the circumstances, I doubted it would be about my job performance.

Mr. K. Much like his wife, Mr. K got straight to the point. He asked if I knew what a printer's devil was. I told him it was usually a young man who was an apprentice working under a master printer, or printers. He liked my answer and replied, "Did you know that Mark Twain worked as a devil apprentice?" I answered to the negative, "But maybe if I do what Mark Twain did, I could end up a writer like him." Mr. K, wearing a broad smile said, "Let's go, I'll show you the shop."

We entered through the door from the office. It was one step down and we were in a good-sized print shop. I was truly impressed by Mr. K's enthusiasm and dedication to the trade.

He said the writers and editors were in the row of offices you see when you enter through the public entrance. They developed stories, editorials, police logs, weather reports, and local news. "These people are the other half of our team," Mr. K explained about the print shop.

He went on to describe the *very mechanical* Linotype machines. "The operators reproduce in the lead alloy slugs the exact copy of the writers' submittals. The slugs in turn get arranged in trays, side by side, until they are large metal pages. The final template is sent to the printing press people."

Mr. K was obviously proud to say his small shop was capable of casting solid lead alloy ingots in a template capable of printing hundreds of local newspapers each week.

I took the job and soon realized more of my new job revolved around attending to the Linotype operators and maintaining the shop than writing or editing. It was hard for me to understand how Mark Twain did it. I spent as much time with the broom as I did setting type. The glamour went out with the waste from the crucible.

For the next stop in my tour included being introduced to Harry and Bill, the two linotype operators. They were comfortably seated in front of the large machines at attached keyboards. They put into metal type whatever news articles came in from the writers.

They were master printers and as I was soon to learn, unusual characters. Bill was in his late 40s. He had a great sense of humor. He was an avid scuba diver and as Harry put it, "He went too deep for too long."

Harry, however, was in his mid-30s and a spirited individual. He liked to drink and smoke, whatever came his way. A blink into his past showed that Harry learned printing during a stay at Colorado State Prison. It seemed Harry had an affinity for guns and motorcycles that some might see as unhealthy.

Both men were accomplished tradesmen who worked hard and played hard. They were loyal to the newspaper and to the owner. Mr. K said, "Although a little rough around the edges, they got the job done, regardless of any problems or deadlines."

My first day, the following Monday, I showed up for work right on time. Harry had a coffee waiting for me. Bill was on the Linotype machine but took time out to greet me. Before Bill returned to setting type, he swung around and said, "I am in charge of this shop and for everybody who works here. Harry and I have a real good thing going because we work together and have each other's backs." I got the message!

Harry told me later to relax and do what I was told, and how I was told, and things would go fine. "You especially have to do things the way we tell you. We deal daily with machines and devices that don't discriminate between your fingers or a piece of lead type. The machines will stamp out either one."

Bill added, "Do you see those heavy gloves hanging next to the crucible? They protect your arms up to your elbows for a reason. If you accidentally get splashed with even a drop of the molten lead, tell us immediately so we can get medical help." He continued to explain that hot lead will burn you and cause severe infection and probably lead to poisoning.

I listened very carefully while Harry led the tour, basically showing me what my job was. I didn't know at the time that these would be the last totally serious conversations our small team would ever have.

As time went by, I realized what Mr. K meant about getting the job done. Amid all the kidding, swearing, and verbal jousting, we always got the job done on time. I recall many afternoons sending out to Antonio's for pizza, then working into the night.

Oftentimes when we were in the thick of trying to meet a tedious deadline, one of the front office people would come flying through the shop door in a panic. They were often waving their arms and shouting profanities.

This usually meant Mr. K had just cut out or changed someone's story. These episodes usually took place just as we were finishing the last pages, or what we called the galley manuscript. Bill always handled these outbursts with a volley of his own refined profanities, but the problem always got solved, then and there.

When you have a small three to four-person staff that is under constant stress and often overworked, you can predict dysfunction. This breakdown can eventually result in a gradual disintegration of the core team. This condition leaves the team open to industrial injuries and other collateral damages.

Just to be contradictory, our small team grew closer and, in many ways, strongly protective of each other.

The worse the stress at hand, the tighter our bond became. There was a shared suffering, something common in the human species.

We weathered many hectic challenges during my apprenticeship and a few hair-raising episodes, many times involving Harry. His love of guns, or better stated his love of shooting guns, was usually in the mix somewhere.

There were several incidents that took place that were not necessarily as reckless and dangerous as they were bizarre.

It is this writer's choice to share two such incidents for the sake of clarity of character. Both incidents expose very extraordinary events taking place in very ordinary settings.

Mrs. K's Surprise Birthday Party

One such incident took place at a very beautiful and tranquil rural setting. It was Mrs. K.'s surprise birthday party. The gala event was held at the K's lake house on a nice sunny afternoon. The entire staff, family and friends were all invited. The mixed crowd seemed to get along fine, especially following a few cups of fruit punch.

All was well with plenty of food and liquor for everyone. Harry and I kind of moseyed around the crowd and finally landed on the rear porch overlooking the lake. We could see across the lake to a beautiful stand of evergreens that descended down a hill and ended at the water's edge.

Harry and I found ourselves perched in two comfortable porch chairs with our feet resting up on the porch guardrail. As we were sitting and chatting an oversized horsefly continued to fly from beer bottle to beer bottle. We both could see and hear the party crasher trying to get at our beer. Each time either of us waved it away it would buzz around our heads in a threatening pattern.

Then it made a crucial mistake. When Harry waved it off his beer it flew directly at him landing on his forehead.

Harry was not the type of man to take such an offense lightly. He instinctively tried to swat the attacker but instead was only able to slap himself in the forehead with a loud thud. I was going to laugh out loud but gave it a second thought when I saw the expression on Harry's face.

I instead asked, "Did you get the dirty little rascal?"

"No," said Harry, and he went on to say, "This showdown is not over!"

With that, the fly once again landed at the top of Harry's beer, as though mocking him. I told Harry in a laughing voice to take it easy, it was only a dumb fly.

Harry then turned to me saying sharply, "You stay out of this kid, nobody does that to me and gets away with it!"

Then in an instant Harry swung around like a true gunfighter and pulled out a 22-caliber pistol. He then squeezed off two shots at the fly taking the fly and the top off the beer bottle.

I sat there in disbelief of what had just happened. With a satisfied smirk on his face, Harry calmly turned toward me and said, "I got the dirty little bastard."

Then with a twinkle in his eye he put the gun back in its holster. He proceeded to grab another beer from the cooler and put his feet back on the porch guardrail. He acted as though nothing had happened.

Out of the house came Mr. K and a few guests wondering what the two loud popping noises were. Harry quickly got up and was pointing in a frantic manner shouting, "Where did those kids go?" As he pointed across the lake. "They ran out on the dock across the lake and threw two loud firecrackers into the water. Did anyone see them?" Harry put on a magnificent act.

With that, Mr. K looked at Harry as though he could see through him and said in a suspicious tone, "There is something fishy going on out here. What the hell is that sulfur smell?" Once again Harry was the lead actor saying, "It's the cheap Italian cigar George is trying to keep lit."

After a while we wandered back inside and had a big piece of birthday cake with a few more beers.

Mrs. K mentioned that in all the years they had owned the cottage it was only recently that they noticed any questionable activity in the area. Harry replied, wearing a large smile and said, "You know Mrs. K, it just isn't right the way this younger generation acts out at times." Mrs. K nodded in full agreement, then thanked us both for coming to her party.

Before we started our motorcycles, I asked Harry if he thought he got the fly. He laughed saying, "I'm pretty sure I whacked him with my second shot, anyway. I don't think the scuffle did him a hell of a lot of good."

Harry and the Cannon

It was a late Friday night, and I was trying to hurry through my shop clean up when I heard a motorcycle pull up near the front entrance. I cautiously walked over wondering who might be visiting here, so long past business hours. I was the only employee who stayed late on Fridays.

When I walked through the office area, I could hear someone with a key opening the front door. I stepped a little closer and realized it was Harry. He came bouncing in with two cold beers sticking up from the right and left pockets of his leather riding jacket. He declared that it was officially a beer break.

It was hot on the whole first floor of the building from running the crucible earlier in the day. A nice cold beer sounded great. Harry asked if I had shut down the Crucible and cast the remaining lead. I told him I had and was closing the shop down for the weekend.

Harry seemed to have something on his mind, so I cautiously inquired, "Harry, what the hell are you up to now?" He simply said he bought a cannon and that I was going to help him figure out how to cast cannonballs. I laughed until I realized that he was dead serious. I had flashbacks of the fly on the beer bottle episode earlier in the summer and thought it best to play along with him.

He said that he bought the solid brass miniature cannon in an auction for $100. It was an exact replica from a civil war cannon later used as a deck gun on British frigate ships.

The barrel and its mountings were also perfectly to scale. He went on to explain how the manufacturer sealed the first three inches of the barrel as well as the small hole at the other end of the barrel that would facilitate a wick.

Harry went on to say that the auction had been online so it would be a day or so until it arrived. I have to say I felt a little relieved when he told me about how the barrel was leaded up for public safety reasons.

Then it all became clear to me. He was going to impress me into duty. I was about to become his munitions contact. When I said out loud what I was thinking, I said it laughingly. Harry didn't crack a smile.

When I felt his response across the room, I recalled similar incidents when I made light of his proposals also keeping the fly incident and Colorado State Prison in mind.

We adjourned directly to the back room where the Crucible and lead ingots were stored. Harry picked out the top ingot in the stack, still warm from being cast earlier in the day. He looked at me with a smile and said, "What's a couple of cannonballs between old buddies." I didn't reply but thought to myself, *I'm not an old buddy, and printer's devils do not cast cannonballs in their time off.*

I told Harry I had to finish cleaning the front offices. He thought I was trying to avoid talking about his future plans for the cannon. He couldn't have been more correct. I knew then that he wanted an accomplice in getting the cannon to fire without blowing himself up and everything around him.

His original idea was to buy a few boxes of tennis balls and cut holes in the tops. Then, with my help, fill them with molten lead. The only fault with that plan was the hot lead would collapse the ball and spill out. To randomly spill molten lead is very dangerous. Agreeing that the tennis ball cast was a reckless idea, he bade me goodbye. Just before he got all the way out the door he turned to me and said, "It is early, and we don't have to work tomorrow. Meet me at the Fox and I'll buy you a beer." The Fox of course was one of his favorite watering holes. "Don't Worry, you don't need an ID in there." I agreed to join him.

I finished my clean up and headed down for a beer break.

I knew Harry's plan was to prime me up with a few beers then get me involved in his crazy cannon project.

When I arrived Harry already had a cold beer waiting for me on the bar. I was doomed!

As soon as I sat down, he began making small talk chatting about our motorcycles. 15 to 20 minutes and 3 beers later Harry then casually turned the subject from our motorcycles to work. He told me how well I fit in, as though I had been there for years. Then, into our 4th beer, he sprung the question.

"George, with all your skill at handling hot lead, do you think we could design a cast and rough out a few cannonballs. I could do the finish work at home."

For some insane reason the whole project sounded great! Maybe one too many brews that's something to do with it.

In taking my last sip, I spun around on the barstool like John Wayne used to do in old cowboy movies and said, with great resolve, "Count me in pardener!" I later hoped they wouldn't end up to be my famous last words.

We had another beer and shared a few ideas on how to make a durable cast. We needed one that could hold up against the hot lead. We had some good ideas but we both agreed that we should do a little more research, behind a lot fewer beers.

The next day was Saturday. I was sure my brain would function better when it had time to dry out. Sure enough, later that day I suddenly remembered that Mr. Lintz who lived down the street from me used to work in one of the several foundries that once operated here in town. I was sure he could help with our cannonball project.

Mr. Lintz was an elderly man of German descent, probably in his mid-80s. His daily routine was to ride his bicycle or walk to the Community Center several blocks from his home. There was a senior lounge and cafeteria where he met with other seniors to play pool and have lunch.

I was certain if I went there I would have a good chance of meeting up with him. When I drove by, I spotted his red bicycle in the bike rack out front.

I went in and found him sitting in the small library reading the newspaper. When I approached him, he smiled through his bushy white mustache and asked how I was doing. I replied that I was doing fine and went on to tell him about the cannon and if he had any ideas.

Mr. Lintz paused for a moment and in a jovial tone he said, "I think that after being in the foundry business for more than 30 years I can certainly cast a cannonball or two."

He went on to tell me about some ancient casting techniques called lost sand casting. It amounted to making an impression in the sand the shape of your item and slowly filling it with your choice of molten metal.

Mr. Lintz was a wise old man, and it was plain to see he very much enjoyed explaining the casting method, and in much more detail than was needed. He also asked if I would share with him how things work out. I in turn asked him if he would care to join us, he promptly answered with a firm "No!" He went on to say, and in not so firm a tone, "George, you are a hell of a nice guy, but I don't want to share a jail cell with you."

The next day I called Harry to tell him of my findings. He was excited and said, "Guess what, my cannon arrived yesterday, and it is all they said it would be!"

Unbeknownst to me, Harry had already made plans for us to meet at the print shop next Saturday to work on the cannon barrel and try our hand at cannonball casting. I was now fully aware that this project was actually happening, leaving me with a case of the vague uneasies.

All week long, Harry made no mention of the cannon he kept concealed in the trunk of his car. I paused for a moment and gave that picture a reality check. An ex-con riding around Wallingford with a cannon in his trunk. At this point I was almost hoping he had forgotten about our partnership.

As Friday afternoon rolled around, once again, Harry was chomping at the bit to get back to his project. He twice mentioned to me about possibly meeting in the shop at 8 a.m. on Saturday. He was quite anxious to get started with the actual hands-on work required to make the cannon functional.

Our first task was to remove any restrictions inside the cannon barrel. It would take skill and patience to successfully remove any blockage without destroying the inner surface of the barrel. I couldn't believe it, but I was getting caught up in Harry's aura of excitement, sensible or not.

Saturday morning quickly rolled around, and I was ready to jump into the cannon restoration business. As much as I always put a negative spin on the project, there was on some level a boyish fear and excitement that piqued my interest.

As I entered the shop I saw Harry with his back to me. He had his work apron on and had set up a temporary light over the workbench. He was bent over working on something or somebody in front of him under the light.

I couldn't help remembering a similar scene from an old Frankenstein movie. When I got closer, I saw there was no cadaver on the bench, but there was a very well-made cannon sitting there. It had a wooden base with four wheels on the underside, like those below-deck guns on old pirate ships.

When I got closer, Harry heard me and spun around to greet me. He said, "Isn't she a beauty?" I quickly responded, "Yes, I can't wait to get started."

Harry claimed he had drilled and ground most of the lead plug out of the muzzle of the barrel. Once the obstruction was removed, he could lower the small sanding head into the barrel to clean up the rough spots.

A cold chill came over me when I asked Harry why the barrel was set in the heavy wood frame. He responded very matter of factly, "Well, this way all I will have to do is remove the wheels and then bolt the cannon and base directly onto the wood framed forward deck of my old cabin cruiser." Coincidentally the old wood boat was named The Captain Morgan.

It suddenly became very clear to me that my uneasiness regarding the project was not at all unwarranted. I was participating in the creation of a 21st-century pirate about to be set free in Long Island Sound!

At this point I was secretly wishing that Harry would scrap the project, or that some outside power or event would let us both out with limited collateral damage. I couldn't picture this happening. Now I could better understand Mr. Lintz's concern about getting directly involved.

With all of that on my mind I quickly returned to reality. There it was, a scaled down real cannon anxiously waiting to sink the first Chris Craft that crossed her bow.

Harry looked at me and said, "You look like you've seen a ghost." He went on to brag a little about how he was able to drill the plug out of the barrel without damaging the interior surface.

We chatted a bit about our next task which was the casting of the cannonballs. While we talked, I casually slipped my question in.

"So, Harry, when the hell were you planning to tell me about the mounting of the cannon on your boat? I didn't even know you owned a boat. Don't you think that having a cannon mounted on your forward deck might attract a little attention?"

Harry chuckled at my questions and in a very sincere voice replied, "George, don't look so worried. I'm only going to use it for duck hunting."

He went on to explain how ducks often land as a flock along the salt marsh areas. You would be lucky to get one shot off before the whole flock panics and all fly up at once in different directions it was Harry's intention to get up as close as he could and ready the cannon.

I quickly learned that making a cannon ready is a general term for arming it. This would entail adding gunpowder and then cannonballs, a wick and whatever else the individual cannon might require to be ready to fire at the captain's order.

For Harry, getting the cannon ready would include placing lead pellets, called birdshot, into the cannon. This would enable him to effectively fire into a whole flock of ducks. He presented this explanation to me without batting an eye. He simply wanted to take down 20 ducks instead of just one at a time.

I completely understood how as a duck hunter your dream might be to shoot down a whole flock of ducks at once. But what about the need for cannonballs?

Harry turned toward me slowly and said, "George, thanks for reminding me, let's pour a few while you are still here."

With that we adjourned to the "hot room" where the crucible was kept. Our next job was to try Mr. Lintz's suggestion and utilize the lost sand method for casting cannonballs. We adapted the method a little and began pouring lead.

The deeper we got into the project the more bizarre it appeared to me. To our surprise, Mr. Lintz's method worked well. In less than two hours we successfully poured 4 nicely round cannon balls.

I ratcheted up my nerve and asked Harry point blank what he was going to do with our four shiny projectiles. He hesitated and said, 'I didn't think it would be effective to use them for offshore deer hunting. I'll just use them for target shooting."

I was sure at this point in the game that I wanted to get out of this partnership. For the second time I prayed that I could get out and not destroy my friendship with Harry. I decided I would just screw up my courage enough to look him straight in the eye and tell him exactly how I feel.

He was just finishing the final sanding of the rough edges off the last cannonball when suddenly before I could state my piece he began saying in a very sincere tune, "You know George, I really appreciate your moral support with my project. Most people would think I'm nuts and leave. I really appreciate your help."

We sat down drinking beer and kidding about what would happen if we pulled the Captain Morgan into the Newport Yacht Club with the cannon, bright and shiny, mounted on the bow. I was hoping our kidding didn't give Harry any ideas. My only saving hope was that the old boat wouldn't make it all the way to Newport.

Just before I got out the door Harry shouted, "I am almost finished with my first close range heavy timber target. I will let you know how my first test comes out." He kind of hinted that he preferred doing the first test firing alone as he put it, "in case I blow myself and everything around me to hell." He wasn't kidding!

Sunday morning rolled around. I got up and checked my phone for the time and weather. Suddenly the screen flashed a previous call from Harry at about 1:00 in the morning. He left a message telling me that the first Test of the cannon didn't go as well as he had hoped, and could I meet him at the shop around 8:30 a.m. He sounded like he had probably drunk down the last six pack before he called. I headed over on my motorcycle about 8:00 AM. I sensed trouble in the air.

As I pulled into the parking lot, I saw Harry's motorcycle parked alone in front of the shop, and then remembered it was Sunday morning.

When I entered the front door, I could hear the murmuring of the loud sound of exhaust fans. This was not a good sign.

Harry hollered, "That you., George?! Come on down into the shop."

When I walked in I could not believe my eyes. There was the cannon tethered to the shop setup table. All the shop chairs were covered in dust along with every other flat surface in the area. I sensed again that something wasn't right. As I entered, I walked by our large worktable, there was Harry wearing a big grin and holding a cold beer in his hand. Then I looked to his right, and I couldn't believe my eyes. There was a two- to three-foot wide hole through the back cinder block wall.

Harry turned to me and in a serious tone said, "The cannon works great but I think my aim was off to the right a little bit."

I anxiously replied, keeping in mind that my job was hanging on a string, "Harry, what the hell are you talking about, that your aim was off. You blew a hole through the shop wall."

He just laughed and told me to calm down and have a beer. I took his advice.

He explained that yesterday, after I left, and a few beers later, the thought of putting up a plywood target seemed very logical. Placing the target over an open window was also a great idea. The target would theoretically slow the cannon ball. If the cannonball went through it would be out onto the lunch patio and then into a stand of medium sized trees. "What could it hurt?"

As the story goes, the cannon was roped fast to the setup table, then Harry lit the wick and ducked. The cannon fired just fine but recoiled to the right. Rather than hitting the plywood target it blew a hole through the back wall, cracking and crushing several of the hollow cinder blocks. There were hundreds of small pieces of mortar and concrete strewn about the shop. The mess also spread through the wall to the lunch patio right outside the large gaping hole.

Harry said it was quite a show. The cannon gave out a loud blast of flame then recoiled to the right, missing the target and resulting in the obvious renovation to the back wall.

Henry explained that the hollow masonry blocks did not offer much resistance. The lead ball blasted through the hollow blocks and came out the other side.

Unfortunately, it retained enough velocity to effectively decapitate the boss's new gas grill. It sat on the lunch patio about one foot from, what used to be, the back wall of the shop. But the target survived untouched, still nailed over the rear window, about three feet from the hole.

Right about then Mr. K came bellowing through the door. Aside from the stream of profanities, he made it clear, "You are both fired! I trusted you both over the years together. In one single Sunday you take to testing cannons in the rear of my print shop!" Mr. K went on a rampage shouting, "You both are liable for blowing a part of my back wall out, causing a layer of dust and cement chips to cover the shop, and blowing the top off my new gas grill!"

Mr. K then ordered that the shop and outside lunch patio be cleaned. He also told Harry that the wall would require temporary and permanent repair. As far as the grill goes, "Since it was a gift from Mrs. K, you can deal with her," he said and stormed out.

With that Harry and I cleaned up the shop and patio. Harry took the plywood target from the window and used it to neatly cover the gaping hole in the wall.

It was a very quiet clean up. Harry proposed that we schedule a meeting with Mr. K and Mrs. K to plea bargain for our jobs. I agreed that we should be proactive. I wondered to myself how many people began their full-time job careers this way.

Later that evening Harry called to confirm our meeting with both owners in Mr. K's office at 9:30 sharp the next morning. We both knew we would need a miracle to get ourselves out of this mess.

Monday morning at 9:20 we were both standing outside Mr. K's office like two grade-school kids waiting to be seen by the principal. The trial was about to begin! However, Mrs. K couldn't make it. She was in some manner a big wig in the local historical society, and she had to chair their monthly meeting.

Mr. K silently opened his door and invited us in to have a seat. There were three chairs set up but fortunately one of the jurors was absent, and she was not missed.

The boss began by saying, "Let's hear what insane excuse you come up with for firing a cannon off in my print shop within two blocks of the police station."

Harry quickly took center stage. He began by expressing in great detail the fact that George (the Devil) had nothing to do with firing the cannon or assisting in any way, shape or form. His closing statement was, "I take full responsibility for the incident and take full responsibility for my own reckless behavior."

Mr. K was truly touched because he genuinely liked us both. He said, "What could possibly make you think it was alright to pull such a stunt, and how did you ever think you would get away with it?"

Harry replied, "I bought the cannon at a gun traders auction specializing in 18th century firearms of all kinds, including disarmed cannons and Gatling guns."

In addition, he added, there were several of these miniature cannons manufactured as showpieces used by the cannon manufacturers to show prospective buyers. There are 10 to 20 more of these still in circulation. This specific model was duplicated from the on-deck cannons serving the frigate ship Penelope. This was a British naval vessel well known for its many maritime adventures.

It was plain to see that Harry caught Mr. K's attention. With that, Mr. K suggested that we adjourn to the shop to do some damage inventory. It appeared that Mr. K might have an alternative agenda.

When we entered the shop, Bill was at the Linotype machine. He swung around sensing there was trouble in the air. He laughed and said, "What's up guys? Is something wrong, I had nothing to do with it." Mr. K replied, "No, we just want to investigate your buddy Harry's arsenal."

Harry stored or hid the cannon under the same set up table that had hosted his one-cannon salute Sunday night. It was completely wrapped in old newsprint paper to hopefully go unnoticed.

He carefully unwrapped it and set it up exactly the way it had been when he fired it. Bill, not knowing the whole bizarre story, jokingly shouted, "Hey boss you aren't going to fire that thing in here, are you?" Nobody laughed.

Harry went on to show the boss the fine details, including the forward wheels. The closer Mr. K looked it over the more interested he became. He and Harry went on investigating and exchanging questions and comments. Harry's manner took on all the characteristics of a used car salesman.

The next step included a review of the specification manual and the historical background of the full-size cannon. The literature that came with it reviewed in detail where and when the cannon was manufactured. It explained that Harry's cannon was a duplicate of the cannons made for use on the frigate ships, circa 1800s.

The reason HMS Penelope stood out in history was because of its commission to hunt down and capture slave ships. It was also one of the first frigates to be converted from sail to steam power. In the process the ship was reduced in weight by using deck cannons and employing lighter-weight cannons below decks.

Our cannon was an exact miniature of the new deck guns. This makes the miniatures valuable for contemporary collectors and prized as the only models of the new artillery available during the 1800s. Also as expected there was no historical accounting for using them for duck hunting or deer hunting.

It was plain to see that the boss had a genuine interest in Harry's cannon. It might have been Harry's many history lessons on the British maritime or maybe the slave trade that caught him off guard. I began to wonder could this episode possibly save my first real job? I had a glimpse of hope!

Then came my second glimpse of hope, to our surprise Mr. K simply turned to Harry and asked him if he could buy his cannon! We were both stunned by his sudden change of heart.

What could possibly interest Mr. K enough to buy the cannon that just blasted a hole through his shop wall and wrecked his new gas grill? Then Harry chimed in saying, "Mr. K, you know I have been a good and dependable employee over the years. You hired me as an ex-con when nobody else would talk to me, and I will always respect you for that. So do you think maybe we could put my reckless behavior behind us, and you can keep the cannon?"

Mr. K then took a hard look at me, then gave the same look to Harry, then a look at the cannon, then back to Harry, then stroking his chin he said, "I tell you what, you get the wall repaired, on my dime, I keep the cannon, and you and the Devil go back to work."

"Deal!" Harry quickly replied. "George and I will be back to work Monday and thank you!"

Mr. K smiled and I felt as though he was looking for a reason not to fire us. He went on to say, "Harry or George, please help me carry the cannon and the cannonballs out to the front office." He muttered, "I assume the extra cannonballs are part of the deal?"

"I'll throw them in for free if you promise to be careful with them," Harry replied.

Mr. K scowled and handed me the ammo to carry to the front office.

Mr. K instructed me to leave the cannon in Mrs. K's cubicle. He smiled and decided to take the cannonballs with him. It was finally beginning to seem like the crisis might be coming to a close.

It was Monday morning and Harry was tapping away at his Linotype machine, the mason was about finished repairing the wall, and I was putting together an ad on the infamous setup table. We suddenly heard a ruckus of a woman laughing and crying out from the front office, "Thank you! Thank you!"

The mason was the first to inquire and he waved us to come and look what was going on around Mrs. K.'s cubicle.

Harry, Bill, the mason and I peered into see Mrs. K crying out, "Oh, Gilbert, you must be the most thoughtful, great husband in the world, to first remember my birthday and second to find the perfect gift!"

Two other silver-haired elderly women were definitely some sort of "cause people." Harry mentioned something about being Daughters of the American Revolution, although neither of us really knew what that meant.

When they spotted us they called to us to come and look at Mrs. K's wonderful gift. One of the old dolls excitedly pointed to the cannon and said to Harry, "Have you ever seen such a perfect antique, and just imagine if you could see where it has been and what it has done?"

Since Mr. K was standing directly across from the room glaring at us, neither Harry nor I responded, but just smiled.

We were then asked to carry the canon out to Mr. K's car. As I passed Mr. K, he quietly grunted, "If either of you ever whispers one word about all this you are automatically refired." I quickly replied with a smirk, "Our lips are sealed."

As they lifted the cannon onto the back of Mrs. K's vehicle, I took the liberty of asking what she was going to do with it. She turned and said, "For years I have been searching hard to find a suitable donation from our family to the Historical Society's small museum in the town hall. This cannon is perfect!"

As she glanced back towards me in a suspicious tone, she asked, "George, is it my imagination or does the muzzle of this beautiful little cannon have a cap gun or sparkler smell to it?"

I casually replied, "Oh yes, every cannon produced by this 1800s French manufacturer was closely inspected and tested prior to putting them out into the marketplace."

Mrs. K. smiled again and replied, "Of course, how authentic." Harry was standing close enough that I could see his eyes shoot straight to the top of his head in disbelief of my comment. I told him later, "I had to say something. Kind of like you did that time at the lake about the boy lighting off firecrackers."

Mrs. K. left and I said, "Well Harry, this should lock our jobs in for life," as I strutted by with a smug look on my face. Harry sharply replied, "Okay professor, now what the hell do we do with the boss's blown up gas grill. It's still out on the patio."

* * *

It should be noted that in addition to the less than normal antics that were highlighted in my story, the work team at the job was second to none that I have ever experienced.

Once a week this team produced a small-town newspaper. The final product was the result of a well-disciplined, hard-working group of people. They took pride in their work and taught me the same by example. I learned how to work and more importantly, I gained Harry as a friend.

Chapter 7
The Good Old Days

I could feel the repeated tugging on the big toe of my right foot. It was my new best friend Yaz. Our remotely activated wake-up system worked. He called it our "personal mobilization system." He loved the military sound of it.

Yaz was only 10 ½ years old when he devised his silent and dependable method of getting me out of bed at 4.45 in the morning. Yaz needed help with his steadily growing newspaper route. This was a big deal for two upcoming entrepreneurs, plus it was a dependable source of spending money. Yaz's personal mobilization system required a long length of string to be tied to my right-foot big toe. It was mandatory that we secure the big toe closest to the bedroom window. The communication line, as Yaz called it, would be lowered out the window height Yaz could reach. He bicycled up the block at 4.45 a.m. He would then proceed to give three good yanks on the communication line. Three tugs was the code for Yaz. This system never failed to rouse me for work. Work for us included packing up, folding and delivering over 65 newspapers before school started at 9 a.m.

The schedule had been much too hectic for Yaz to do alone. When his route reached over seventy customers, he hired me to help. We found that we worked well as a team. This resulted in a 60-40 partnership that lasted over two years. And so began the adventures of two young men growing up in an old industrial area of a town during the late 1950s and early 1960s.

Although Yaz came from a more financially sound family than I did, we both lived in the same dark-blue-collared neighborhood. There were factories at each end of our street. Single and multifamily houses along each side shared the common sidewalk — end to end. The entire neighborhood had a steel mill, two silver factories, and a wire company mixed in with the playgrounds, schools, and a small park.

I often heard my mother complain that on certain days her wash hanging outside would look a little gray and smell of smoke. Our end of town, or neighborhood, was a mix of nationalities, races, and religions.

I don't recall any evidence of discrimination in our school or on the streets. What I do dearly recall are the ethnic aromas coming from Mrs. Torres's, Mrs. Torello's, and Mrs. Yescott's kitchen as we were walking home from school.

I knew that if we wandered into Mrs. Torello's kitchen with her favorite grandson, Anthony, we might get a piece of Italian bread to dip in her tasty sauce simmering on the stove.

All this being said, our family landed in one of the three layers of poor, but we didn't know it until we got older and out of school. There were several unhealthy and physical dangers all around us, but we survived.

We learned early on that if you worked, you would have money. This led us to delivering newspapers, shining shoes, washing dishes, raking leaves in the fall and shoveling snow in the winter.

Since Yaz and I now had full-time, part-time jobs, we became a bit more independent.

We could buy candy and a few bottles of soda, cigarettes, and even afford a 25-cent matinee at Wilkinson's Theater. I remember our first summer working. Yaz got a flat tire on his paper delivery bike. We would usually end up at Chick's Junkyard, or the dump, in search of a junk tire or inner tube. We felt that we were really something when we marched into Maliguti's Bike Shop and bought a brand spankin' new tire and tube.

We had come a long way!

Mechanically sound bikes were mandatory to get us uptown to the newspaper office by 5.30 a.m. Once again, this is where our personal mobilization system came in handy.

The simple method always worked unless I forgot to tie the communication line to my toe, or it accidentally slipped off during the night. Once awake, I would quickly clean up, grab my jacket, and quietly get on my bike and head uptown with Yaz.

He was always glad to see me. Maybe it was because we were friends or maybe because he would remind me each day what a great invention his personal mobilization system was.

We weren't aware at the time that our abbreviation, PMS, might stand for something else.

I would always agree and remind him, "Yaz, if your system didn't work, I wouldn't be here to agree with you."

From our house, we could bike in toward the center of town. Along the way, we would always stop by Mabel's Luncheonette to check and see what kind of donuts Jimmy, the owner, had ordered for the day.

His daily order of doughnuts and breads was always in neat white bags in his covered doorway. We usually took two doughnuts and left 25 cents for each. Our next stop would be in the downtown cemetery. There were a few comfortable benches in the shady areas along the older tombstones — behind Mr. McAuley's was our favorite spot.

We would sit and smoke a cigarette or two and eat our doughnuts. Then, we would continue pedaling up the hill that runs through town and to the newspaper office.

The hill seemed extra-long and tiring going up, but steep and fast on our way down. Once at the newspaper office, Barry, who worked distributing the unfolded newspapers to the carriers, would hand us our stack for folding.

There were usually six or eight carriers in the same large room. We would all be folding the loose newspapers into squares, hopefully to fling onto our customers' front porches. It was easy to determine which carriers were the pros by how quickly they could fold the papers.

It was amazing to watch a few of the senior carriers in action. They were faster and neater than the rest, and they knew they were. I wonder if Freud and his gang knew how folding newspapers in a rather dingy room with six or eight fellow folders could promote self-esteem and self-worth. When we completed folding our 65 papers, along with a few extras, we packed them into two large canvas carrying bags. Then we tied them to our bike baskets by the long shoulder straps on each bag.

Our next move was cycling down Center Street Hill as fast as our loaded-down bikes would carry us. We always tried to get the morning papers to our customers before they left for work. Most of our tipping customers took our extra effort into consideration when we got paid. An extra 10 cents or 25 cents was a big deal. We also made a point to leave our extras for a few of the poorer families.

When we dropped off the last few papers, there was still time enough to get a good breakfast before school. Yaz pulled into Cox's Market. We proceeded to pick up something we could eat at their picnic table alongside the store. Yaz bought some Twinkies, a Coke, and a delicious looking cream-filled donut. I preferred the twin pack of Hostess cupcakes, a Coke, and a small blueberry Table Talk pie. I agreed to split the pie with Yaz because we had to eat and run, literally, to get to school on time.

School wasn't too long of a run or bike ride from the store, meaning, we might still have time to stop at the old walled cemetery for another smoke break.

In recalling those early smoke breaks, I remember that we didn't inhale cigars or cigarettes until much later in our smoking careers. It was excitement of the whole procedure rather than the intake of nicotine that attracted us. Also, if you smelled of cigarette smoke walking into the school, other kids might think we were cool or tough guys.

We played around a lot but we were always respectful to our teachers and most of our fellow students. Yaz, the Kraut, and I only got sent home once for fighting three students from Simpsons School on the other side of town.

The fight was broken up by two teachers. Even though it happened on our way home, the teachers reported us to our principal.

After school we could race to Mabel's Luncheonette to play the pinball machines with some of our paper route money.

Jimmy, the owner, paid off high scores from $5, $10, and $20 if you could score high enough. It seemed as though payoffs were very seldom. There were only two machines so we had to get there as soon as we could after school. About 4 p.m. we had to be home to do chores. There was always something that needed to be done inside or outside the house. I knew my mom and dad needed help, especially since my dad was partly disabled. They both came home tired after working all day in the old factories they called sweatshops. That name was more than appropriate, especially in the summer.

My jobs were lawn mowing, hedge trimming, and cleaning up after our old dog, Lassie. Mom always commented about how good a job I did as she was preparing supper. Our family did not have it any easier or any harder than most of the other families in our neighborhood. I am sure being aware of this took a little of the sting out.

Our supper schedule varied, based on when mom finished cooking. Nobody ever complained about her timing since she worked all day too. We all helped. including dad. Dad occasionally made comments about mom having to work because of his disability.

We always ate supper together. Our meals were very basic and good. After supper we all helped clean up the kitchen. I was usually awarded the garbage detail. It didn't take too long for us to get everything picked up and put away. This left some time after supper to relax.

In the summer, while it was still light out, we would sit on the front porch. Almost all the houses on Bull Avenue had front porches within shouting distance of each other. This made for a chatty hour or two.

Many of the neighbors went for walks after supper. There were always greetings and, "how is so and so," or, "did you hear about the Perillo's new grandson?"

Around Thanksgiving Mr. DePalma shared his newly tapped homemade Zinfandel wine. He and his family made wine every year or two. Mr. DePalma thought it was the best wine they made in many years, due to the great California grapes. Each summer two or three of the families grew vegetable and flower gardens. There was no shortage of tomatoes, cucumbers, or squash anywhere on the block.

During this break after supper the kids on the block usually got together in the empty lot between our house and the Camiri property. Our favorite activities were softball in the summer and touch football after Labor Day. Mr. Camiri would often joke that the little lot got as much action as Yankee Stadium. There couldn't be any hanky-panky going on so close to the parents on the porch. The Kelly kids who lived down the street about 15 houses would sometimes have beer and cigarettes except when playing on our lot.

My brother, Bob, and, along with most of the kids on the block, fought with the Kellys on several occasions. If you happened to walk by their house and the four Kelly brothers spotted you, there was a 50-50 chance you would be fighting one or all four of them.

They were not a friendly bunch. Regardless of the altercations that occurred in our neighborhood, we eventually managed to get along, even the Kelly kids stopped the random punching. As time marched on, which it does, with or without us, we graduated from pinball and a not inhaling venue to the old pool hall venue and inhaling a variety of legal and illegal vapors. Yaz and I learned how to shoot pool over our summer vacation. It was not nearly as expensive to shoot pool as it was to learn to shoot pool. The hustlers were expensive teachers.

Eventually, Yaz and I retired our old string-to-toe system for alarm clocks. We were young teenagers and had to be at school by 7:45 a.m. This change of schedule caused ripples in our old, established school commutes. Some changes that initially seemed unimportant later proved to be problematic. The new schedule shaved 15 to 20 minutes off our travel time to school. This meant cutting out some or all of our cemetery smoke breaks. We still had to walk or bike from the far west side of town, across the tracks, past Mabel's, up the Center Street hill, past the cemetery to school.

Not having time for a donut break at Mabel's or a full smoke break in the cemetery threw our whole gang off balance. This led to less than healthy attitudes. The questionable attitudes resulted in less than perfect student performances. This left us with bad attitudes and plenty of people to fight with.

Our only reprieve was we were getting out of school earlier. Since none of our guys participated in any after school clubs or sports, we were able to meet at our new hangout earlier. Stars Pool Hall and Duck Pin Bowling Alley were the locations. Louis Banini, who owned and operated the pool hall and bowling alley had one major rule: no fighting indoors. There were no minimum age requirements for anything. Rowdy or drunken behaviors were not tolerated. Louis occasionally had to throw people out physically. It was nice to have a place to go to after school, or during school. We had a meeting place to relax and maybe shoot a few games of eight-ball.

Once in a while there were big money games going on. We were allowed to watch or bet but had to keep the noise to a minimum. There were many hundreds of dollars changing hands as the result of one shot. These games would occasionally go on all night. The scene was directly out of the movies, or particular movie, *The Hustler*.

As we grew older we would often meet at the pool hall at night and just talk or basically hang out. It was an environment where most were accepted with very few conditions. Many street and living skills could be learned from the various characters that used the place as their base of operations. Fifty years ago, there were not as many drugs or guns on the street as there are today, but booze, cigarettes, and gambling were readily available.

During these formative years we survived living in a very challenging environment. It was often dramatized by comparing the living dynamics of our town to those of an inner city.

It was in such comparisons that our town was described as being in a unique niche, one octave of the blues above the South Bronx. A very colorful snapshot.

We learned earlier on what a real fight looked like and blues, what they sounded like. We were taught how to keep our mouths shut and what it really meant to mind our own business. Such awareness could benefit anybody in any social setting.

Many of us kept part-time jobs to supplement our families' home expenses and have a few bucks left as spending money. Yaz and Big Nose increased their paper routes to well over 100 customers each. They agreed to split the town east and west of the railroad tracks.

Louis Fall, the Fatman, and Jerry Pie, worked in local car repair shops. T.K. and Banana Mike worked as grocery store clerks in wholesale warehouses, and Kraut in a print shop.

These jobs, unfortunately, steered many of us away from pursuing a higher education. Luckily, some of us landed in the trades. Many of such apprentice positions eventually led to personal licensures and the development of small private businesses.

Yaz and I remained friends through the years. He joined the Air Force and got stationed in Utah. I went to college and became a high school biology teacher. We both got jobs in Wallingford, Connecticut.

Yaz was the health director and helped run the local VFW.

I met Yaz one night at a poker game. We hugged and drank a beer or two and talked a long time about the good old days.

We made a promise that we would take a ride back to the old neighborhood and do so soon. It was good for both of us to revisit our roots and remember those who helped us along the way. We revisited the rough spots and the high points of our younger days.

Neither of us had smoked for many years. We laughed when recalling how much emphasis we allotted to smoking and drinking.

Much of our growing years would probably sound strange, dangerous, and even ridiculous to the newer generations.

In many cases, we simply hung out in various places. We occasionally would share a bottle of cheap wine, smoke a few cigarettes, and talk through the night.

We learned how to communicate our joys and fears with safe and close friends. Between our school days, part-time work, full-time work, the military and, for some of us, Alcoholics Anonymous, we constantly socialized on one level or another.

Some of us followed our involvement with organized religion, while others retreated from it completely. Both tendencies were usually attributed to our upbringing, good parental models, sexual abuse, drugs and alcohol, or war. The older we got, a third tendency poked its ugly head out of the mix, having an awareness of our own mortality, or, in simpler terms, a healthy fear of dying.

At age 79, here I am, a brand new, fresh-out-of-the-gate story writer. I know that I am only part-time at my new interest, but I have quickly fallen in love with it. I spend long hours sitting back with a coffee and recreating the various events in my life that I had experienced. It is a luxury afforded to few."

When reading my own writing and traveling back in time many decades, I see some seemingly great events diminished to much less importance. I see minor events inflated to very important, and in some cases life-altering. In some instances, the tedious and lackluster tasks proved later to be character-building.

Maybe if everyone was lucky enough to share in a common task like folding newspapers each morning, they might improve their ability to work and socialize with others. Maybe those psychological bumps that occur along the road to manhood might be softened and appear less frightening.

My childhood through teen years can never be recaptured. My early teens might have included meeting friends around Mr. McKaley's tombstone in the cemetery to sneak a smoke or shooting a game of eight-ball with the Fatman or TK—but I was not alone, and better yet, I didn't feel alone.

The short stories offered in this book may not have dramatic or exciting endings. I simply share a few snapshots in my life. The day began with my big toe being pulled and many years later remembering how grand a time I had and I am still having.

I can still smell the aroma of Mrs. Torello's red sauce simmering on the stove. It was one of the most wonderful smells my world might ever know.

Chapter 8

The Gnat Man Arrives

It was one of those warm September nights when it was too nice to stay inside the bar playing gin and too late to hit Yonkers for the Daily Double.

So, what was a young, red-blooded American lad like myself supposed to do on such a fine night?

I was hanging around in the front of the joint having a very serious talk with Jake and the Fatman. We could not decide whether to bet the over or the under on Sunday's Cowboys game.

Just as we were about to go inside for a cold beer, along comes the Gnat Man. He was one of our boys, and always good to run with. He usually had some colorful scheme in the works. He was accepted as one of our group as a stand-up guy.

You might ask how someone ends up with a nickname like Gnat Man? Unfortunately, there is no dramatic background or superhero story involved in his getting that name. Over the years, all our boys ended up with nicknames. Names that we accepted for life.

In the late summer of 1966, we were driving back from visiting friends and relatives in the South Bronx. It was not an uneventful visit, but still a nice visit. We considered it a good visit if we all came back without a stab wound or someone shot.

On our way back, we always stopped right outside the city for supplies. We bought cigarettes and Ripple wine. Knowing ahead that there would be arguing about whether to get red or white, we bought six ice-cold bottles of each. That would be enough to get us home.

It was a warm night as we cruised cool in the Jakes Brothers' 1957 Caddy. It was a comfortable ride, to say the least. There was plenty of room for all four of us. Once out of the city, we cracked the windows a few inches to let the fresh air in, and the cigarette smoke out.

Looking down a few white Ripples, the Gnat Man's, real name Lewis, verified the quality of the ride by falling asleep in the back seat. Somehow, he must have spilled some wine on his jacket and shirt.

The stains went well within the four or five cigarette burns he had accidentally acquired attempting to smoke, drink, sleep, and join us in our a capella version of "In the Still of the Night."

Jake pulled into our usual, second pit stop, a little Italian pizza joint named Papa's Pizza. Papa, who was Angelo, and nicknamed Chicky, was a middle-aged Italian character who was known to bet the occasional horse race or football game.

Our plan was to make a quick stop for a pepperoni pizza and a few cold beers. We needed to restock the beer cooler for the remainder of our trip.

When we left the car, Lou was still sleeping, so we left the rear window open, like you would for a mutt. Jake thought that was a very nice gesture.

On our way to the takeout counter, Fat Man spotted an older model, two-flipper, numbers pinball machine. We ordered three beers, a pepperoni pizza, and a roll of quarters, for the numbers and bingo machines.

Papa/Angelo/Chicky handed Fat Man the roll of quarters, and he headed for the machine. Jake, being a little curious, asked Chicky what the payoff was on the machines. Chicky quickly replied, "Since there is nobody else in my fine restaurant, for you boys I will make an exception. I will pay you five dollars for the bingo and a buck a game on the numbers machine."

"That's a deal," Jake said.

Chicky added, "And certainly three gentlemen like yourselves would not turn in an old paisan like myself for illegal gambling."

He explained the machines are for the amusement of his customers as they wait for their pizza.

Needless to say, Chicky had a well-stocked inventory of excuses for having the two pinballs and two quarter slots. The slots were hanging off the back wall between the restrooms. Chicky claimed he didn't want the noise from the machines to ruin the Mediterranean ambiance for those dining in his three booths. That was why he hung the "for fun" slots a little out of the way. Fat Man thought that was very thoughtful of Chicky.

Fatman was quite familiar with these older machines, having served his apprenticeship on Jimmy Ped's Luncheonette back in town. You could buy ice cream, subs, burgers, and candy there, and could make a bet on any horse running in the continental United States. Jimmy was a true multitasker.

Once again, Fat Man came through. He started racking up ten games at a time. It was pleasing to watch a true professional at work. By the time our pizza was ready, he had enough to pay the tab. Jake went up to the cash out, or I should say the takeout counter, and picked up the beers. Upon leaving, Jake whispered to Chicky, "Don't worry, Chicky, your secret is good with us," and we left.

As we approached the car, our dear friend Louis was still sleeping. He did have a rough night in the city. When I looked closer through the window, I could not help but notice a lot of old-looking spots on Lou's face.

We looked closer. It was not an everyday occurrence that one of our boys broke out in black spots. Jake looked closer to find that the black spots had legs and were moving around. The black spots were not a skin problem, but a fly problem.

The tiny gnats and flies must have smelled the wine Lou spilled and flew in the open window. When we opened the car door, they all started flying around Lou's head, like one of the old Dick Tracy characters.

From that day forward, Lou has been known in our network of friends as Gnat Man. It is 40-plus years later since that famous event, and the name is here to stay.

We all got back in the car, juggling two six-packs of beer and a free pepperoni pizza. Lou woke up and yelled, "What the hell are all these flies and gnats doing in the car." He quickly blamed their presence on the strong smell of the pizza. None of us commented.

Finally, Gnat Man replied with a wide smile, "So Gnat Man, would you care for a piece of Chicky's pizza and a cold beer?"

The Gnat Man smiled and grabbed a beer.

Chapter 9

Our Home Game

It was six o'clock on a normal Friday morning. There were no neon signs or smoke signals to warn me that by 11 o'clock that night I would be half drunk, half beat up, and all the way in jail.

Since I was a senior at Lyman Hall High School in Wallingford and working part time. I was allowed to arrive 15 minutes late for home room. We also had a designated smoking area. At age 18½ I considered these privileges to be major steppingstones into manhood.

I got my usual 6:15 pickup for school by TK in the 1953 Chevy sedan his father had left when he died several years earlier. We were all very fond of it. As our buddy Jake used to say, "She's no crackerjack, but she's steady, and has a great radio."

Being, the last to be picked up meant I got the backseat between Banana Mike and Richie, also known as "Thing." We were all arguing over the words to the old song, "Louie, Louie," when Yadoots asked, "Is anyone interested in getting drunk before the big game tonight?" Everyone raised their hands, so the motion passed.

During those early days of drinking, I do not recall anyone voting no to such an exciting invitation. There seemed to be an aura of manhood reflecting off the "yes" vote. Although I had never experienced the aura prescribed to be a "no" vote, I feel safe in assuming there were very few manhood credits involved.

Our plan was the same as usual—if nothing else, we were consistent. It was true that our plan was etched in stone, but certainly not the cast of characters that consistently wove in and out of each event. Typical of the 1960s, many of the characters were also making a very visible social, political, or spiritual statement. They were very complicated people in very complicated times.

The first step was to procure the booze. Yadoots would have Old Black Bill pick up a case of beer and four bottles of ripple wine, two red and two white. Two bottles of each gave us a choice.

On occasion, Bill would have some homemade shine. One quart of the "White Lightenin'" would get us all drunk. Plus, we liked the idea of supporting our local, small-business people.

The next step was to drive to our favorite party spot. It was naturally camouflaged and hidden in the woods. There was an old logging road, which led to a beautiful open field, well known for keg parties and bonfires. It was a beautiful hayfield on private property. Nobody bothered us there, not even the cops. It was not a place that anybody accidentally happened upon. If you were there, you were there to party.

As we slowly pulled into the field, we ran into Big Nose and Banana Mike. Big Nose got the nickname because of his long, pointy nose. It kind of resembled a greyhound dog with its collar too tight.

On this one night, we were the only drinkers up there, leaving us with nobody to mooch more booze from. We did manage to drink all we had and were still somewhat sober.

Big Nose and Banana Mike, who worked for Chiquita Banana Company, had to leave early so they could be on time to play in the traditional game between Lyman Hall and East Haven High. Banana Mike always prided himself on proper preparation for these events. He said he had only smoked four cigarettes all day. We were all proud of him.

We were down to our last beer, so we decided to share it. Since Big Nose and Banana Mike had to leave, it left fewer of us to share.

That's when Richie pulled out four little shooters of Jack Daniels from his camo-coat pockets. It was like Christmas all over again. Everyone agreed that warm beer and sour mash whiskey went well together. We were ready to clean up our trash but noticed that the trunk of the old Chevy (a 1950s model) had assorted beer cans and bottles in it. I guess while we were drinking and singing the last lines of "In the Still of the Night," Big Nose policed the area. He thought he was smoky the bear or one of Nader's Raiders. He was constantly picking up trash and bottles along the roadside for recycling. TK said we should tolerate his shortcomings because nobody is perfect. We closed the trunk and headed for the game.

A little over half drunk and a little over half rowdy. We made it to the gym parking lot without hitting anything or anybody. Two of our boys, Gnat Man and Jake, met us there. They also had been drinking earlier at the pool hall.

As we all headed toward the gymnasium doors our beloved vice principal Mr. Fitzsimmons met us head on. His nickname was "Skunky Fitzsimmons," attributed to very distinct stripe of white hair extending from the front to the back of his head. He knew us all very well and proceeded to explain that if we made one false move, he and gym teacher Blacky Richatolli would find us and personally throw us out. Both he and Blacky were very capable of doing so, but they would have to catch us first. Of course, none of us said anything except "we hear you," said more out of respect than fear.

When we stepped into the gym, away from Skunky and Blacky, Jake informed us that the word on the street was that there was going to be trouble. It seemed there was a gang from East Haven that announced out loud that they were going to kick our asses, along with anybody who tried to get in the way.

Word got out that they were specifically looking for some trench coat guy called TK and his biker buddy Yadoots. It was rumored they were in a brawl outside the Spot Café in Meriden a while back, and the payback to those two was going to be a bitch.

Once inside the gym, we could see that the visiting loudmouths were the Easties gang from East Haven. TK pointed out the three members who had jumped him and Yadoots about a year ago. As he recalled, it went poorly for them, especially after one of them ripped the left lapel off TK's trench coat. They underestimated TK and Yadoots.

When we took a closer look we counted eight or nine of them This event was slowly taking on all the characteristics of a full-scale teenage gang war.

Following a brief meeting in the gym foyer, we decided since we were dangerously outnumbered we should stay scattered about in the crowd. If we weren't identified as a gang, we might avoid a bad scene on our home turf.

Of all the members of our gang the Easties knew only two of us, TK and Yadoots. We agreed if they start something with either of our guys, we'd come off the bleachers.

At this point, we realized that some of the Lyman Hall students already knew about the infiltration by the rival gang. Some of our team and cheerleaders were getting heckled and threatened from the sidelines as they entered the gym. Of course, once Skunky and Blackie were made aware of their unacceptable behavior they would hear about it then and again after the fight.

As the game began, we noticed that the East Haven crowd absorbed three or four of their gang. However, the core group was still very loud and visible. They especially heckled Banana Mike and Big Nose, obviously someone had identified them as two of our boys. Considering the booze in combination with the adrenaline rush and the heckling, the fuse was lit. It was official. It was a go!

As the game progressed into the final few minutes, TK unexpectedly burst into attack mode from the bleachers, his trench coat streaming behind him like Batman's cape.

That was it, we all charged out onto the court with him. It was game on! The fight began in the main entrance of the court and proceeded through the exit doors. The East Haven gang didn't know what hit them. Even Donnie "the Rodent" Benini joined in. At last count, they had two men down and three deserters.

Suddenly, there were cops coming in from all directions. Everybody was still punching, and yelling. A couple of our boys flew off the bleachers from a different angle and took two more Easties out, then bolted out the side doors. They were both on probation, so they had to "hit and run."

By this time, the game was officially over, and there were crowds of students and spectators flowing from the bleachers. The on-duty faculty and cops picked out six students in the confusion, mistaking them for gang members. In the midst of this mess, the last of the fist fights were still going on. The total chaos helped our boys to flow out with the exiting crowd.

Once outside, we all walked inconspicuously to the parking lot.

The remaining East Haven gang members also realized that it was time to beat it out of there. Between the public, the students, the gang members, and the cops, there was complete disorder and confusion. This made our getaway a little easier.

After the crowd had thinned out the entire gym was now visible. There were three spots of blood and the collar from someone's shirt left in the middle of the gymnasium floor. Fortunately, only one spot of blood was from our boys. Yadoots took a direct hit from two opposing gang members ending up with a cut lip, a black eye, and a shirt with no collar.

Four or five of the Easties got picked up by the cops—Skunky or Blacky—as they pushed and bumped their way through the crowd.

Surprisingly, none of our boys got nailed by Skunky or Blackie. It was helpful that the Easties kept the faculty and the boys in blue very busy.

All of our gang were to meet at the Star pool hall downtown. Everyone showed up, except Yadoots. Although the mad rush of cars provided perfect cover for our cars, it didn't work as well the one motorcyclist, Yadoots! Adding to the problem, it was pretty tough for him to explain his cut lip, black eye, and collarless shirt to the cops.

Louis Benini, who owned the pool hall, knew the sergeant on the night desk at the police station. He agreed to call the sergeant in search of Yadoots but nothing more.

Sure enough, they had him in the holding cell, and his missing collar in a brown lunch bag at the front desk as evidence.

The sergeant also told Louis to call back a little later. "I should know by then if we are going to book him or let him go with a warning."

We had some time to go, so we decided to shoot a game or two of eight-ball while we rehashed our recent victory. Even Donnie the Rodent added his piece.

To our surprise, Louie indirectly told Donnie, his son, how he felt about street fighting when he said, "I'm not encouraging any of you to break the law, but sometimes a man needs to stand up for himself." It looked like he was staring straight through Donnie when he said it.

After about an hour or so, TK handed the phone to Louie, who agreed to call the station back. The sergeant reported that Yadoots had been released to his father's custody. The sergeant, knowing the old man, added,

"The station came very close to being turned into a wild west show."

The sergeant said further, "It finally ended in the showdown between the four young patrolmen, the old man, and the kid, Yadoots."

The sergeant told the four young patrolmen, after they released Yadoots, "that they didn't know how much trouble they were lucky enough to have avoided." He continued to say, "If the old man thought that any of us laid a hand on his kid, it would have taken more than you four rookies to take him down."

He went on to tell Louie. "Luckily, the kid took full responsibility for his part in the incident and was truly sorry for causing worry to his parents. As strange as it may seem he could not remember any names of anyone else involved."

Then the sergeant said excitedly, "Wait Louis, you have to hear this, there is more." He went on to explain how, just before the patrolman was about to hand the kid over, the old man whipped around, faced the officer, and said in a cold voice, "Son, how did you get that cut lip and the black eye? Did any of these guys put a hand on you?"

Luckily, the kid told him no, that he'd been fighting and would explain the whole thing later.

The sergeant admitted he felt very uneasy until the kid came clean. He continued, "I do suppose I rushed things along following the kids' surprise statement. I just wanted to get everybody out of the station before the whole episode started over again."

He went on to say in a much calmer voice, "At About 11 p.m. I quickly handed over Yadoots and the brown lunch bag with his ripped shirt collar in it. But it wasn't over yet!"

Another surprise to everyone in the station was when the old man pushed the kid out the door and thanked the sergeant.

When the old man could see the kid was in the clear outside he bade the cops good night and continued to cautiously back out the door.

Louis said the sergeant was still quite excited when he said, "Louie listen to me, I saw the old man in action in a full-scale brawl at his shop picnic last summer. This showdown could have ended up as bad as that, or worse. This was not a TV special. I'm totally glad they are all out of here. Collar and all."

Soon after Louis completed his call to the sergeant, we heard a motorcycle outside, and sure enough, into the pool hall rode Yadoots. He didn't look so good wearing a major black eye and a fat lip.

His first words were, "You guys aren't going to believe this story." Then TK or Jake tuned in, "We know the whole story about you and your old man. The sergeant told Louis over the phone that he had the cops in a bit of a panic, until he retreated, walking backward out the door."

Yadoots said again, "I had two or three of my best lies ready for him. But when I left the station, I began to realize that the old man really showed up for me, unconditionally. It was obvious that he was willing, while sober, to kick ass and call roll."

The Rodent stood up with a raised voice and said, "Hey Yadoots, we all know your old man pretty well. So now tell us what really happened when he got you in the car alone. Did he bang you around a little or just a backhand and a few threats?"

TK followed with, "Let's hear your great surprise ending, and I hope it's good! This story is beginning to sound like one of those old John Wayne movies."

Yadoots yelled, "Listen, listen, I will tell you the rest of the story, but it's not what you think. When we left the station, he followed after me in silence. I felt like Dr. Doom was behind, marching me to my execution. We got in the car and silence prevailed for the first part of the ride. Then dad barked out, "What the hell happened? You better have a good explanation for the black eye and the messed-up lip after all the boxing tips I handed down to you."

"I explained to him," Yadoots said, "that I got spun around by one guy and nailed twice by some big geek. But I managed to do quite well after that. We did win the fight after all! Dad looked much better after I said that. He finished up by saying in a low monotone, "Remember what I always told you. In a one-on-one fight there is no excuse for allowing any non-pro fighter to hit you more than once in the face." He then smiled and added, "You did okay, son, but next time I get called to bail you out of the pokey, I'm going to tell them to leave you there. Agreed?"

"Agreed," Yadoots said.

Then the old man said, "Let's go home so you can get your motorcycle. You probably can't wait to meet with whatever is left of that rat pack you run with, so you can exaggerate everybody's role in the 1964 Battle of Lyman Hall High."

They laughed together, but that's exactly where he went.

Chapter 10

The Seven-Minute Mile

It was a warm May evening in sleepy Wallingford, Connecticut, a typical laid-back, middle-class, New England town . . . NOT!

Old White Hair was the bartender and owner of the Silver Fox Café. Proud Clarion had just won the 93rd running of the Kentucky Derby, paying $62.20 to win, and all was right in the world.

Proud Clarion was a 30-to-1 long shot, which meant most of the local bookies might have had only one or two payouts. White Hair and his partner, Wayne, were in that profession and had only one winner and all bets were taken. Since the intake of the money was in the hundreds and the total payout was only $62.20, as the local bookies put it, White Hair and Wayne baked a cake.

The clientele of the Silver Fox, or the Fox as the patrons called it, was varied. The crowd was made up of ex-cons, cops, ex-cops, professional gamblers, pool hustlers, alcoholics, a few hippies, as well as a few local professionals thrown in for good measure.

On this one Saturday afternoon in May, one of the three Tartaglia brothers, nicknamed Balloonhead, or BH for short, was watching the news on the overhead TV. He was waiting for the Red Sox score having bet the game. Prior to announcing the professional sports results, they listed the regional high school and college finals. One of the reports included field and track events.

Evidently, some high school kid had just run a seven-minute mile to win a sophomore race. The coaches were pleased considering this was the first track meet of the year.

They interviewed the young man regarding his training and daily living routine. (The runner emphasized a good balanced diet, daily exercise, proper sleep, and of course, no drinking, drugging, or smoking.)

In the meantime, Smitty and Joe D. were in the high-stakes gin game, which was normal. Gambling was a common day and evening pastime, which included any legal or illegal way to make money without working. Thinking back, there were not very many clean-cut, hard-working average American men in that lot.

The list of the characters could go on and on, but for this story we are paying attention to Balloonhead. He delivered beer for a living and was proud to say he was a card-carrying Teamster. He often bragged that he alone delivered up to 300 cases of Budweiser beer in a single workday. It was truly an astounding show of physical strength and endurance.

When not delivering beer, he would be drinking it, and smoking. Other pastimes might be playing poker or gin at the Fox. On off days, he might be at the golf course or the local pool hall. He was surely a multi-talented man, and at heart, a good man.

The Fox had an unusually high number of local hustlers and con men. Many of these men were fine-tuned masters of their craft. They took their skill sets very seriously, and a few of them even weaseled their way into politics. The Silver Fox Café was similar to a finishing school for hustlers, gamblers, and scam artists, and the occasional politician.

But on this one Saturday evening, May 6, 1967, an event took place that is hard to appreciate without having been there. It is equally hard to write about, considering the bizarre details of the event. The involved characters didn't think that the episode was anything out of their ordinary, which covered a lot of territory.

As the bar had settled down, following the Derby, White Hair and Wayne had collected all their winnings and were buying a few rounds of drinks for the boys.

In the midst of all the usual noise of pinball and rowdy behavior, BH began to loudly critique the track and field events that followed the derby. He shouted over the crowd, "That kid only ran a seven-minute mile. Anybody could do that with a few days practice."

The words that went down in Silver Fox history were, "I'll bet anybody in the joint $100 if that punk kid can run a seven-minute mile all duded up with track shoes and all, I can run a seven-minute mile in my work boots and Teamsters uniform!"

Everyone gradually got in on the argument until YaDoots and his sidekick, the Kraut, threw $100 on the bar saying, "BH could run a seven-minute mile as is."

Bingo! White Hair and Wayne being assertive businessmen, yelled over the crowd, "We will book any amount of cash that BH can run a seven-minute mile with his work boots on or off, we don't care if he runs in his underwear!"

Four the next half hour or so the joint was jumping and money was flying in all directions. It appeared that the early betting made BH the favorite, but they couldn't figure out where the event could be held. The next question was who did they trust enough to measure out the mile and keep accurate time?

Then Billy and another Teamster, suggested holding the event that night to shut BH up once and for all. He pointed out that one of the finest quarter-mile tracks in the country was right here in town, at Choate School, a private prep school.

The final plan was for everyone to meet at the outdoor track just before dark, so none of Choate's people could be in our way.

It was agreed that post time was 7 p.m. BH added, "If we all drive up from here we could light the track with the car headlights."

It was a great plan so long as the night security guards didn't show up. Then it would be every man for himself. It was settled.

At 6:30 p.m. a convoy of six cars and one motorcycle headed across town to Choate School. BH had only one beer and didn't smoke for three hours in preparation for the race. As BH put it, "With all this money being bet, I have a responsibility to take this race seriously." We all arrived at the Choate track and field complex and drove up onto the grass area surrounding the track. White Hair and Wayne directed the cars to strategic spots along the oval where their headlights would be of most use. The scene was set.

Very few of the spectators, bettors and runners had ever seen a well-manicured quarter-mile track. They were much more familiar with horse racing tracks. One of the spectators named Milo, a cook at the Fox, wanted to know where the starting gate was.

The whole gang was there and getting anxious for rave time. Although not quite dark, by the time the crowd gathered around the finish line, we knew the lighting would be of good use.

One of our guys brought along five or six small folding chairs for the seniors in the crowd.

The three voluntary late entries to the race surprised us all. We now had to set aside time for them to get their bets in. Tricky D and Wildman were entered as 10 to 1 shots. The last entry, who was nicknamed Thing, came in at 20 to 1. The two bookies had finally collected all the bets and were ready for race time. Among the long shots, a crowd favorite was Wildman V. It was well known that he had outrun the cops and his ex-wife on several occasions.

None of the entries had ever been on a real track. When told they had to go around four times to equal a mile, one anonymous entry tried to back out, but it was too late. The bets were all in.

In rethinking the scope of the event and seeing the entries, the idea of setting a few simple rules seemed appropriate.

The following terms were agreed to and read aloud by Wayne. Number one, no eating speed prior to the race. Number two, no physical contact among the runners—no punching, pushing, or tripping, especially along the poorly lighted stretch. And number three, no threats of physical harm between runners or spectators.

After hearing the rules, or terms of engagement, the bookies in the crowd thought it might be wise to present the following guidelines for the spectators and their customers. Number one, no throwing any solid objects at or in the path of passing runners. Number two, no threatening runners with bodily harm. And number three, any known bribery to fix the race would immediately disqualify the involved runners and nullify any bets.

The rules made perfect sense to all involved. It was a well-informed group.

As the runners were preparing for their event, White Hair and Wayne appointed themselves as timekeepers and final callers of the race. No one opposed. There was total trust.

All agreed that the beep of the unique sounding motorcycle horn would officially start the race.

Once again, another start-up delay. One of the runners had to urinate and put his cigarettes in his car.

The race was finally about to start. White Hair made his call to the runners, and Yadoots hit the motorcycle horn on cue, and they were off!

Heading for the first turn, Tricky Dugan took the lead tight on the rail.

In second place was Wildman, who also cut to the inside from the start. The rest of the pack followed by four lengths.

Coming down the back stretch for the first time, it was still Tricky D ahead of Wildman V by three lengths. Unfortunately, from there on, we couldn't be sure of positions due to poor visibility.

As they came down the stretch for the first time, Tricky D still led Wildman V, BH began closing the gap, and Thing was setting himself a slow pace.

The next two laps ran basically without incident except for BH. He had tightened things upon their run down the back stretch. BH was leading at the top of the third stretch by four to five lengths. Wildman V and Tricky D were now trading second place back and forth.

As some of the bets were on Wildman V, Tricky D, and Thing, betting one against the other, in the last lap, the excitement shifted from BH to Wildman V and Tricky D. They were battling it out as they approached the last lap. Passing the finish line for the third time, it was BH by eight to ten lengths. It seemed as though BH had saved his kick for the final lap. Behind him by several lengths was Wildman V with Tricky D trying to close the gap between second and third. Thing was still a distant fourth.

As all four runners passed the finish line for the third time, the crowd cheered for the three long shots and booed BH. The fact they all four had lasted three full laps seemed to amaze all that watched.

Into the last lap, the crowd was up on their feet waving and cheering. They all passed the spectators heading for their last run down the backstretch.

As they hit the final backstretch, BH was far in the lead. His work boots began kicking up the track as he accelerated again. At the same time, Wildman V and Tricky D were also going into the back stretch — it was close!

Both were bearing down. Thing was several lengths behind and fading fast.

BH was coming off the backstretch to the top of the final run, pouring on the juice. If he could pick up the pace through the stretch, he might possibly beat the seven-minute challenge. It's the final run for the money.

Down the stretch in the middle of the track came BH whipping and driving as a jockey would put it, pushing hard for the home stretch. He crossed the finish line in six minutes and 47 seconds and the crowd cheered, though most had bet against him. As he passed the finish line, he fell on the grass, exhausted. He needed a cold beer.

In the meantime, Thing fell forward toward the middle of the backstretch to rest a bit. At the same time, Tricky D and Wildman V started down the home stretch just feet apart, both giving their final kick. The crowd went wild!

As they passed the finish line, it was Wildman by two lengths. "He closed like Secretariat," some said. Tricky D finished only a few seconds behind but never quit.

Even Thing picked himself up and finished the race at his pace. The crowd closed in on the finish line, cheering and clapping. They made Thing feel like a hundred-game winner. The crowd had gotten behind the runners, each having their favorite.

Just as Thing passed the finish line, out from the shadows appeared a badge. For this crowd, a badge meant trouble. It was the Choate security guard making his nightly rounds. He obviously knew a few of the Silver Fox boys.

All the athletes were around White Hair's station wagon, having a cold beer and maybe a little tequila. Then there came a deafening silence as the crowd all had eyes on the guard. No one could predict what might happen next.

The guard came close in the poor light and Milo recognized him. It was Chuck, an occasional patron of the Fox. Milo yelled, "Hey, Chuck, good to see you! You want a beer?"

"No, never on duty," Chuck said. "I take this job seriously."

White Hair in a friendly voice asked him how he was doing. Chuck replied "Good, I just have to make sure there are no trespassers on Choate property."

White Hair replied, "You know, Chucky, some people have little or no respect for other people's property."

Chuck's last reply was, "Well, everything looks in good order here, make sure you tidy up before you leave — soon."

Off Chuck went without looking back. We picked up all the beer bottles and one empty tequila bottle.

Soon the caravan managed to meander its way down the hill and across the railroad tracks. There was a serene, sincere aura of camaraderie in the group.

When we all resumed our regular seats back at the Fox, an individual cheer was given for everyone involved. It was unusual for all these characters to cheer for each other.

Just as the last cheer went up, in the door walked Chuck, the school security guard. White Hair asked how he was doing as he opened a beer. Chuck said, "It was an unusually quiet night on campus so I thought I would stop by for a quick beer."

Well, of course, there was another loud cheer for Chuck. Several of the boys said hi and thanks, and the joint settled back to normal, except for White Hair purposely forgetting to charge Chuck for his few beers.

Smitty and Joe D were playing gin at a booth in back, Wayne and White Hair were busy calculating the day's finances, and Balloonhead was watching the sports reports. This report included a swim meet at Yale.

BH said, "I could have knocked 30 seconds off my race time if I didn't have my work shoes on. I'll bet anybody in the joint $100 I could match the time of any one of the sprint swimmers."

This time nobody paid much attention, and as the sun set ever so gently over the railroad tracks behind Gino's Deli.

All felt right with the world.

Chapter 11
The Motorcycle Ride

The music-loving younger generation was watching the Beatles' debut on the Ed Sullivan Show, and still arguing about the words to the Kingsmen song "Louie, Louie."

Also, President Johnson signed the Civil Rights Act and Voting Rights Act into law following an 83-day filibuster in Congress. The Nobel Peace Prize was awarded to Martin Luther King Jr., and Johnny Unitas was throwing winning passes for the Baltimore Colts.

It was around 6:30 p.m. on Sunday, June 14, 1964. I had met a few of my motorcycle riding friends at our favorite pub, Fiddler's Green Café. It was a bright and lively place for those who cared to hang out there. It was also a safe place to drink.

We had been drinking and playing gin rummy long enough to get slightly inebriated and hungry.

Since I had won some money playing cards, I talked two other bikers into making a "shore run." This meant having a couple of shots for the road and biking to the shoreline pubs along Route 1 in Connecticut. We also intended to get a seafood dinner and visit old friends along the way.

The other bikers teamed up with riders, and six of us headed out of town. The night was clear and warm, making riding conditions ideal.

Between Wallingford and the Route 1 pubs, the roads were in good shape but poorly lit. There were several great, sweeping curves, which seemed even greater and more sweeping with a few shots of tequila in us. We all knew the way through the rural portions of the trip, having traveled the route for years.

I had one of my best friends, Johnny D., on the back of my bike. He was used to my riding style and confident in my ability. The three motorcycles and six legally drunk riders were out for an adventure.

When we reached the wooded rural area, the road was shaded by a canopy of tall trees. It was a very beautiful ride as dusk crept in. As we approached a long and straight length of the road, one of the other bikers ran by me as a challenge. This meant a race to the end of the straight-away.

I, being the senior rider, took the challenge and passed rider number one. As I zoomed by him. I gunned it to show how it was done. At the end of this open stretch, an S-turn appeared in the road ahead. This downhill run was also sided with heavy wire-rope guardrails. It sounds very dangerous, but I had run this portion of the road for many years. I was also well aware of what my limitations were regarding speed. I had left the other two bikers quite a way back and began my approach to the top of the S-turn.

I saw the other two bikes in the rearview mirror, and I was sure I had plenty of road to either side of me. I knew I would need the whole road to safely make the curves.

As I leaned into the top of the first turn, I looked down in terror. The Public Works boys had begun sanding and oiling the road from the hill section forward and downward.

My mind switched from having a fun run to one of implementing every riding skill I knew.

As I leaned the bike to make the first turn I began to slide on the oil and sand. It was like racing onto an ice-covered pond. I quickly downshifted and thought, "I can't panic." I had just a split second to think, and I knew my only alternative was to make it a controlled skid and slide onto the grassy space between the road's edge and the cabled guardrail.

I suddenly realized the cycle was out of control and sliding along the slick surface. At this point I hoped to make a controlled crash. The alternative was to crash through the heavy guardrails and down the steep embankment.

Then I looked up — I could not believe what I saw. The Public Works crew had removed the guardrails and lowered the cables flat to the ground. I was headed straight for an opening! To beat that for luck, they had laid the old guardrail posts perpendicular to the roadway, leaving an even easier passage into grassy shoulder.

My body and the bike sailed between the posts and laid the bike into a hard left turn. My only chance was to turn into the grassy trail running parallel to the road or fly off the wooded side into the swamp.

Somehow, I was able to downshift and power through the turn, only to face the remainder of the narrow path.

I remember thinking I was about to crash and possibly die at the speed I was going. I down-shifted again, slowing down as I traveled on this path between the guardrails and the top of the slope.

The next thing I knew, I was at the bottom of the last turn, still not on pavement, but stopped. Johnny D. and I were aboard the cycle, and still alive. The other two bikers told us all they saw was my headlight bouncing, and all they heard was a lot of revving of the motorcycle engine.

They were sure John and I had been badly injured or killed. I had to rest and catch my breath. I saw where I entered at the top of the "S" curve, and the downhill path to where we ended up. Had just one guard post been placed in the path or had a piece of the detached cable caught a muffler or a foot peg, we would have surely crashed! I truly don't remember most of the trip.

The other bikers were amazed we were alive and well. Not a scratch on either me or Johnny! There were many high-fives and congratulations to us as a cycling team for having lived through such a stunt, unscathed.

I repeatedly explained that there was someone or something other than me driving from the time we made it through the guardrail to where we came to rest. My theory was immediately rejected, and I was returned to hero status by the group.

I knew in my heart that something beyond me had happened, but I could not explain what. We then proceeded to the first pub. I humbly took all the credit and free drinks that followed.

We continued to dinner and then home without further incident. But I know to this day that what happened might be judged differently by different people. But to me, it was much more of a spiritual event than a physical event, and for a time, I was not the one in charge of the bike under me.

Chapter 12
Fishing with the Hook

The first question is, can you ever imagine going fishing in a beautiful rural trout pond? The second question is, can you ever imagine fishing in that same Currier and Ives setting with three characters just shipped in from "West Side Story" or "Blackboard Jungle?" Well, this is my story, and one of my many memories of growing up and living around some very colorful people.

Although our boys were not always angels and sometimes had their own interpretation of the law, they did enjoy several healthy outdoor sports. Besides horse racing, they occasionally would charter a party boat for offshore fishing or spend an afternoon clamming along the coast. However, their favorite was freshwater fishing. They might often be spotted fly fishing along one of our several rivers or fishing at one of our local lakes.

Probably the best fisherman in our sports network was Freddy the Hook. He was an old friend and survivor of his early years, as we all were. In adulthood Freddy was what some might call a hard-assed steelworker. He walked steel, as the hardhats put it and he proudly served his country with a hitch in the Navy. Freddy worked hard for everything he ever owned.

He hung out with our old gang since we were all kids on the block. All of us in our unique network had some caliber of nickname, flattering or not. In the case of the Hook, his nickname fit his attitude and his physique.

Hook, whose real name was Freddo or Freddy, broke his arm as a child. The broken bones in his arm never healed properly, so he could only open his right arm at the elbow about 45-degrees and it resembled a hook. Many of his family and friends claim that as a result of long-term physical therapy and weightlifting, the hook arm developed into a lethal weapon.

It was indeed true that any person or object he clamped the hook arm onto was not getting away. His favorite running mate, the Gnat, would often compare his lockdown on a person or object as being similar to a snapping turtle. Once it clamped down on something, you'd have to cut its head off and manually pry the jaws apart. This was Freddy the Hook.

The Hook and Gnat Man loved to show each other up when it came to fishing or clamming. Each season, they would start out on opening day with their rivalry. Gnat Man was able to beat Hook at clamming since he got turned onto this new secret spot. Rumor has it that his good buddy, Yadoots, told him about the spot, although it couldn't be proven. However, it seems logical that Yadoots, a long-time employee of the town of Guilford who occasionally worked with the Shellfish Commission, might know about such a place.

It is also perfectly believable that Yadoots, a dear friend of Gnat Man, would have shared the spot with him. Gnat Man claims he found, "Clam Heaven," as he called it, by himself.

In turn, Yadoots, who was not known as a liar, claims he gave Gnat Man the spot because he was the worst clammer in town. Gnat Man's late father, Goat Man, who was an outstanding clammer and fisherman, was always proud that his son would find such a great spot. Yadoots never had the heart to tell him that a blind man could find clams at that spot.

Since Hook knew he couldn't beat Gnat Man at clamming, he wanted to be sure he nailed him every year in the fishing competition. The last year of them officially competing, Hook brought one of his best catches to Deacon Joe for positive verification.

Although Deacon had a few flaws in his law-and-order resume, his word on the street was never challenged. This made Hook's several catches credible. And similarly, Gnat Man would share his buckets of clams with his friends and several times sponsored a few small picnics on his dime and on his clams. Even Yadoots got invited.

Regardless of the fact that they were very active outdoor sportsmen, it should be noted that getting required licenses and honoring no trespassing or private property signs were not their strong points.

Both claimed that because they fished on private property, no permits or licenses were required. Many of the private ponds they fished were posted by the State of Connecticut, which again, did not apply to them.

On this one starlit summer night, Hook, Big Nose, and Gnat Man were hanging out at their favorite bar drinking and playing pinball. In their limited conversation, Nose made a casual comment about his new trout fishing spot. He explained that as nice as the spot was, he only caught one small trout and threw it back.

Hook quickly replied, "One lousy trout, get real. I will take you to a trout pond that I guarantee you will catch at least four prize-winning sized trout."

Both Big Nose and Gnat Man agreed to meet Hook in front of the bar at 7 a.m. the next day. The only required equipment was that each guy bring his own fishing gear, and for some odd reason, they had to wear a green shirt or jacket.

As 7 a.m. rolled around, up showed both the Hook's apprentices, as he put it. They were both prepared with all their gear and a pint of blackberry brandy. Gnat Man claimed sometimes there are rogue temperature changes in June, so he was prepared with a little internal warmth, just in case. They all together looked more like they were heading for the St. Patrick's Day parade than fishing.

They stowed all their gear in the back of Hook's wagon, and so another excellent adventure began.

When they arrived in the general area, Hook pulled the vehicle off-street and into an old logging trail. Both Big Nose and Gnat Man jumped into a chorus of questions and just plain bitching about having to walk through the woods and where the hell was this great trout pond and what's up with having to dress in green. Hook calmed everyone down with a few pulls of blackberry brandy and a promise that they wouldn't have to hike too far. He described the short hike as a small price to pay for getting to fish the best trout pond in Connecticut.

Gnat Man asked why they had to park so far from your so-called great trout pond. "We haven't seen any pond or trout yet!"

Hook immediately noted a distinct smell of insurrection in the air. He had to think fast. He was very well aware that his small crew was capable of anything at any time, especially if they thought they were getting hustled. He quickly called a stop for a breather, and a brandy break. The brandy worked as always. Everybody was rested and calmed down. Big Nose even said he might have picked up a little buzz.

Hook went on to tell them about the awesome fish they were about to catch. He also suggested that they stop at Deacon Joe's on the way home to drop off a few fish and have a few beers.

Nose was the least suspicious of the two apprentices until he spotted an old wire fence with a no-trespassing sign dangling on one eyelet. To make things worse, a short way along the fence hung a second no trespassing sign. Both signs read "Private Property. Area Patrolled. Trespassers will be fined $100."

Hook quickly told his two apprentices that the signs were meant for non-residents. He also added, "since we are all upstanding Connecticut residents and all have drivers licenses, which count as legal identification, we are cool." He went on to explain there would be a gate approximately 200 feet farther into the woods, and that only residents knew about it. Both guys looked at each other and nodded their approval.

As the trio forged onward along the fence line, Big Nose pointed out that they would be in the big patch of thick woods behind the varsity soccer field at Choate School.

Hook changed the subject pointing to the gate that was coming up around the bend. As they approached the gate, Gnat Man noticed that there was a good-sized padlock attached to a section of chain partially buried in the leaves under the gate. Nose checked the chain and showed where it had been cut off with bolt cutters, a telltale discovery.

There was a clear path from the gate, inland. The path was the rear entry to something or someplace. The crew's renewed enthusiasm overpowered their suspicions, and they chugged forward. However, the clipped chain and the "No Trespassing" sign still lingered in their minds, not helping Hook's credibility.

Hook was once again the fearless leader of the motley crew. It seemed as though the boys could sense the victory of the hunt dead ahead. As the merry band headed up the trail, Big Nose said it reminded him of a similar band of characters from The Wizard of Oz. When Big Nose shared his visual with the boys, Hook immediately took issue with being compared to Dorothy. Nose quickly apologized and suggested they all forget about it and have a brandy break. They all agreed and then went on.

When they approached the entry to the clearing, Hook, for some reason, wanted everyone to stay in the shade of the trail while he went ahead. He was like the point man in a military reconnaissance team. The boys wondered what he was looking for.

Gnat and Nose watched as he scurried up what appeared from the woods to be a small hill or berm of some kind. When he got to the top, he scanned the area and then signaled to come ahead.

When they got to the top of the berm, they knew why Hook smuggled them in through the woods. They realized they were standing on the berm containing the private trout pond belonging to Choate School. It was built and stocked exclusively for the enjoyment of their elite students and faculty.

The pond was so large it could be called a small lake. A picturesque old dock extending 10 feet or so into the pond lay on the other side. It was probably for the Choate people to fish from. The area was well kept and well patrolled, typical of Choate-owned buildings and properties.

Hook finally came clean and confessed that this was his special trout pond that he had been fishing for years. He knew the best time to fish, and when the trout were feeding. He also knew when Chuck, the campus cop, made his rounds. Hook also figured out that when Chuck made his rounds, he only walked as far as the dock, due to a bad knee.

Hook gave the signal to leave the top of the berm and regroup at the bottom. This was to avoid getting spotted by Chuck, who was due by shortly. It was a fact, as Hook claimed, that Chuck or any passer-by could see across the pond from the dock. Anybody fishing from atop the berm would be a wide-open visual target.

Eventually the crew walked, tripped, and slid to the base of the berm. All three fishermen were safe and accounted for. The fishing gear and brandy also made it without a hitch. The lush green grass made a beautiful setting for the gala event that was about to unfold.

As the green-shirt crew mustered around Hook for their final briefing, he explained that their fishing posture was extremely important. If they were to have a successful outing, it was imperative that they follow instructions and copy his example carefully. With that, Hook, spinning rod in hand, walked up to the base of the berm and proceeded to lie on his back. Before the boys could commence questioning, he laid the pole along the length of his legs and sharply cast backward up and over his head into the pond. Gnat and Nose could hardly believe what they were witnessing!

Just as the boys were about to start laughing, Hook hooked into a beauty. He played the catch the same as he would if he were standing on the dock. Nose said, "So Hook, it looks like you must have done this a few times," and then laughed as he put the catch in the creel.

Hook invited the boys to join in. They assumed the position on their backs on the bank of the berm and after a few practice casts and another pull off the brandy, they were ready. All three lying on their backs and casting up over their heads was truly a sight. The whole scheme of events from parking the car off-road, entering through the woods and fishing at the far end of the pond finally started to make sense. If Chuck were to come along, he would be hard-pressed to see anybody fishing using Hook's innovative posture method. Also, it now made sense why green shirts or jackets were mandatory. The green fabric blended in perfectly with the grass-covered berm.

As the day progressed into noon, the trio had all caught several large trout, just as promised. The creels were full, and the brandy bottle was empty. It was time to go. The Hook made the announcement that there shall be no cigarette butts or bottles left behind. Littering after all was against the law!

On the way out, along the wooded path, the conversation was light and lively. They all had a story to share as though they had fished alone. Gnat Man claimed he landed the biggest fish. And Hook, as usual, argued that he had the biggest catch of the day. And Big Nose caught the most and claimed the number caught takes precedence over the size of the fish.

As they were getting their gear put in the car, Hook asked if the crew mind if they stopped off at Deacon Joe's house to share their catch with him and his wife Rosie. They all agreed they could stop there.

Hook added, "If we should get invited in for a beer or two, or maybe a taste of homemade wine, it might hurt Deacon's feelings if we were to say no. Besides, I believe that's what the good Lord would like us to do."

Big nose followed by adding, "Was it the good Lord or Choate School?"

The Hook slammed the brakes on like a madman and said with a sneer, "If I say the fish are a gift from the Lord, that's what they are! Does anyone have a problem with that?"

There was silence. Then Hook resumed driving.

Once again underway, Hook began telling of his secret trout stream. Big nose asked about going there for their next trip. Hook agreed but said in a very matter of fact voice, "Oh, sure, we can all make a day of it, but I will have to blindfold you on the way there and back."

Gnat Man said, "I'm good with that, how about you, Big Nose?"

He replied, "I'll bring the brandy."

And all was right with our world for another day.

Chapter 13

A Red Rose
for a Beautiful Lady

"I've learned that people
will forget what you said,
people will forget what you did,
but people will never forget how you made them
feel."
—Maya Angelou

When I first read this quote by the poet Maya Angelou, I was inspired to write something long, deep, and of course, profound. I guess when you admire someone like a famous author it is only normal to want to be like them.

In my case, I fell short in my first choice of trying to write like Angelou. My second choice was to find an event in my past where I could honestly say my motives reflected her philosophy of people, not forgetting emotions.

My search landed me back in the early autumn of 1964. I had recently been introduced to the "new girl in town." Her name was Ann Canali, and she was originally from New Haven, which is considered to be the pizza capital of Connecticut.

After dating Ann for a short while, I realized that she must have been related to just about every family in her old Wooster Street neighborhood in New Haven.

One of her many uncles worked in Wallingford at the Oakdale Theater. He had worked there for many years and, naturally, his nickname was Uncle Chicky. I say this because it seemed that every family in the Wooster Street neighborhood had at least one uncle or cousin named Chicky.

They all spoke freely about their families and their close family ties. It was always about whose family made the best wine or whose wife or aunt made the best sauce. And with tradition, the age-old argument went on about which pizza restaurant made the best pizza: Pepe's, Sally's, or Modern. There were never any winners or losers declared for fear the arguing might end.

Ann was a good partner and a good friend. Her Italian-American demeanor and looks also helped our relationship. She was my type of gal. She would freely argue with my dad and loved my mom. Dad was not always a good person to argue with and mom loved just about everyone. Also, my mother was half Italian, making her relationship with Ann easier from the start.

One Saturday my mom, Violet Gdovin, invited Ann to come for dinner the following night. This was a sure sign of complete acceptance and a big deal in old Italian families.

While mom was serving baked stuffed shells with homemade meatballs — a family favorite — the subject of birthdays came up. Mom happened to mention that my sister Gloria's and her birthdays were coming up in early October.

The conversation continued through the remainder of the delicious meal. Somewhere in the rather lively exchange, Ann must have heard that my mother very much enjoyed the singing of Wayne Newton. I knew she especially liked Wayne's rendition of his recent hit, *Red Roses for a Blue Lady*.

Dinner ended and we all helped clean up. During the passing of empty plates and the brewing of fresh coffee, Ann asked mom if she had ever attended a live Oakdale show. Mom told her she had gone only once with her friends from the Holy Trinity Ladies Guild. They voted to skip bingo one night and see a show. She said she especially liked the intimacy of the small summer theater. Back then, the Oakdale (which was founded in 1954) was a small in-the-round theater complex, not the large venue that it is today.

As I was driving Ann home, she casually mentioned the idea of setting mom up to see a show at the Oakdale. It would be a perfect birthday gift. The only problem was how to buy tickets. Her birthday was a mere eight days away. After a quiet pause, Ann quickly shouted, "Uncle Chicky!"

She knew Uncle Chicky would get the tickets, somehow. Chicky was famous for saying, "No problem. My cousin, my nephew, or my brother, knows a guy."

Well, this time, at Ann's suggestion, I was hoping that Uncle Chicky might be "the guy" to get us our tickets. I was sure if Ann asked him with her sad face on, Uncle Chicky would melt and tell her "No problem."

When we got to Ann's house, she invited me in to talk to her father. He had an office in the cellar where he worked. Mr. Canali was a great guy whose nickname was Red. He liked me and I liked him. He said early in our relationship, "I'm only telling you this once. Don't do my little girl wrong." I understood what he was saying.

When we got downstairs, Red was just finishing a phone call. I asked him several times what he did for a living, and finally, he answered, "I guess you would call me a kind of self-taught accountant. I deal with numbers all day and try to keep the books balanced." I got that message too.

When Ann told him her idea he smiled and thought it was a great plan. He agreed to talk to Uncle Chicky and take care of the details.

Three days later we had our three tickets for the main show at the Oakdale on Saturday night a few evenings after my mother's birthday. The seats were in the second row from the stage, among the best seats in the house. "Good ole Uncle Chicky," we all agreed.

On this Saturday night, Wayne Newton was doing a special show. His guests were Jack Benny and Rochester, performing in the unique theater in the round. The circular stage was great for the audience and for the singers. It was an intimate setting allowing show people to circulate through the aisles with ease. Ann told mom we had a surprise for her birthday. We were taking her to see Jack Benny at the Oakdale. Since Jack Benny was one of her favorites, she lit up like a Christmas tree and hugged us both. We did not tell her about Wayne Newton. On the day of the show, she rested to be sure she would be in peak condition to enjoy seeing Jack Benny live. She got her gray hair fluffed up by Mary Capucci, who lived two houses down from her. I heard through the grapevine that she bragged a little about the show that night at the Oakdale.

When we all got together to go to the theater, she told dad she was getting all dolled up for her birthday, although a bit belated. Dad commented, "You are still a good looker, Mama." She blushed and off we went. Dad was happy to see her happy, which helped every-one's spirits. Dad was convalescing from a long illness, but I caught him still checking mom out with devoted eyes.

As we approached the theater parking lot, we both kept mom busy so she wouldn't see the billboards and posters along the way. We managed to get to the main entrance talking all the way, without her spotting any sign containing a picture or mention of Wayne Newton.

The summer theater was inside a large round tent, which resulted in semi-permanent six-foot high walls. The aisles resembled the spokes of a giant wheel with the hub of the wheel being the raised circular stage.

The stage was surrounded by the orchestra pit and theater lighting.

A very handsome and smiling usher briskly guided us down to our seats. As we got closer to the stage, mom made a comment that she hoped nobody would fall off the stage and land on us. We undoubtedly had one of the best rows in the house.

We got seated and mom was thrilled with the pre-show excitement. She saw the band members and the stagehands scurrying about adding fresh flowers all around the stage. There was especially an abundance of red roses.

We had 25 minutes to go before the main show started. There were young men and women singing and fluttering about keeping everyone's attention off the main entrance.

Ann told mom she had to go to the powder room, winked at me, and left. About 10 minutes later she was back and gave me another wink as she sat down.

Mom grabbed the program off the seat before Ann sat on it and saw that Wayne Newton was the star singer with Jack Benny. She turned to me, then to Ann on her other side, and said, "Did either of you know about this?" She pointed to the picture of Wayne Newton surrounded by bouquets of red roses.

We admitted, "Yes, we wanted to surprise you."

Mom replied, smiling ear to ear, "If I had known that Wayne Newton was here, I would have gone to Mrs. Antonucci's flower shop and got us red roses for our lapels."

The band then began playing and down the aisle from behind the audience came Wayne Newton. The pit band stopped playing and a New Orleans jazz band, that seemed to appear out of thin air, began strutting in and playing *When the Saints Come Marching In*.

The entire theater began to come alive, clapping and smiling along with Newton, who mom affectionately referred to as that "cutie pie, Wayne."

As the entourage passed our row and proceeded up onto the stage, Jack Benny entered from the other side of the theater, carrying his violin. It was truly a great entrance.

From there on there were songs and violin pieces involving both stars. Then they took a brief intermission. Mom along with the entire audience was loving it.

At the beginning of the second half of the show, Jack Benny barged in on Wayne's first song. He was waving his arms and yelling, "Stop, stop, stop, haven't you forgotten a very important announcement?"

Wayne sheepishly said, "Oh my, don't be mad at me Mr. Benny, I'll do it right away."

Wayne turned to the crowd and announced, "I believe there is a special birthday person in our audience tonight. Where are you, Violet? Mrs. Gdovin, wave your hands so we can all wish you a very happy birthday."

Mom was stunned, but she still waved her hands. Wayne came down the ramp and, on his way, picked a red rose from the stage decorations. He then went directly to our row and said "happy birthday" to mom. He said, "Violet, I have a red rose here, for a beautiful lady."

From there on it was a fairyland as he faced mom and began singing *Red Roses for a Blue Lady*.

There were tears of joy and love in the air. At the end of the song, he handed mom the red rose, wearing a genuine smile on his face. I was sure that no mother's child in the theater that night would forget their mom's next birthday.

The show went on with songs from Wayne smoothly mixed in with the stand-up comedy of Jack Benny and Rochester. Laughter and song filled the theater right up to the grand march out of the tent, led by the two superstars.

The car was unusually quiet on the ride home. Mom seemed pleasantly dazed and was still holding that beautiful red rose that Wayne had given her, as we slowly walked with her into the house. I am convinced the philosophy from Maya Angelou's quote surrounded us in happiness and love.

Chapter 14

Showdowns

When mom heard the cop cars heading for dad's shop picnic, she knew her husband had done it again, the third year in a row.

Once a year, dad's factory sponsored a free picnic for all their employees. It was always held at Wallace Park in Wallingford, Connecticut. The local factories would rent the park from Wallace Silversmiths, which owned the property. It was an ideal location for such events, basically, because it had a large, well-equipped pavilion. And because it was on private property they could serve liquor. In addition, they could also have poker games for those who enjoyed an occasional game of chance.

My dad had gone to work at one of the smaller tool manufacturers in town. At that time, his shop was expanding and working its way up the industrial ladder. Now that it was a successful mid-sized manufacturer, they could afford a full-day picnic with games, entertainment, and prizes for all employees and their families.

When my dad first went to work on the production line — with many other men and women from our strictly blue-collar neighborhood — they were all primarily first and second-generation Italians, Irish, and Polish. As the year went by, the neighborhoods began having large immigrations of Hispanic families. If racial problems existed, I was not always aware of them at the time. It appeared to be a very gradual and peaceful integration. This might have been due to the simple fact that everyone walked to work and school. The only discernible difference between folks was what they carried in their brown bags and lunchboxes.

My dad lived, worked, and drank with many of the local Hispanic dads. My mom walked to the sweatshops with the beautiful Mrs. Torres. But surely the truest proof of integration was many of the Hispanic moms joined the neighborhood women at the Catholic church bingo every Wednesday night.

Although our neighborhood got along okay with the new Puerto Rican and Cuban neighbors, many others from less tolerant local towns and cities didn't.

This attitude was carried into other local factories and Spanish-speaking neighborhoods. This put many of our area employees and neighbors in a tough spot. It was very difficult for them to support the aggressive newcomers during the day and to go to picnics and bingo with their old friends at night.

As time went by, many of the local employees and area residents grew to know my dad as a person to be reckoned with. He had been an amateur boxer and street fighter for many years and had no problem letting the Hispanics, Italians, Poles, and Irish know who he was in more ways than one. It was always the employees from other Connecticut towns that did most of the discriminating and most of the bullying.

One of my father's good friends at work was Larry Donato. He was a mild-mannered sport, small in stature but a giant in kindness.

The newly imported Hispanics over the years gradually became the dominant subculture where my dad and Larry worked. This was true in most of the other factories in the area. As stated earlier, many of them came equipped with a well-developed discriminatory attitude and the gang members to back it up. The active discrimination was aimed toward the established employees regardless of color or creed.

Many of the older neighborhood Hispanics put up with their bullying and intimidation antics in an attempt to stay neutral or invisible. These new and brashly self-confident employees literally became a reality for all to deal with, even the management.

But then there was dad.

He was very well-known by the mixed races and creeds in the factory as well as nearby neighborhoods. Dad's early semi-pro boxing reputation, followed by a few confrontations during coffee breaks, earned him a reputation. Rumors painted dad as a nice guy until you crossed him or forced his hand — then there were going to be serious consequences.

By exploring all the actions, interactions, and covert group dynamics influencing our community, it showed us that violence and fear of violence were strong and influential governing factors. Our basic truth offered a live example of how small communities were often held hostage by an aggressive minority.

These small-caliber terrorist tactics caused there to be silent desperation and fear in most of the residents, except for a few, one of them being my dad. He had individual confrontations with a few much younger gang members causing word to spread through the factory and neighborhoods that the old man was one to always call their bluffs.

Early on there was a showdown between my dad and his friend Larry as they attempted to leave the corner pub. Four or five gang members blocked the doorways.

Paolo, a local gang leader, asked my dad — in a rather demanding way — to go out the back door, dad very coolly responded with, "I hope you let us pass without anyone getting hurt. If you choose to force the issue, I suggest you kill me. If not, I will stalk each one of you down in your sleep, or as you go out to get the paper in the morning or feeding your dog at night, starting with you, Paolo."

Paolo laughed and said, "Let the old fool pass. We will meet again."

Dad replied with a simple, "Thank you," and out he went with the others.

Once out and away from the bar, Larry asked my dad why he said thank you to a thug

"I thanked him for showing us his poker *hole* card," Dad explained. "Grandpa Gdovin always told us to never back anybody into a corner or you will have to fight them on the way out. He thinks he won and will tell everybody in the shop how he pushed us around. There will be another day."

The next week came and went with several different accounts of what had truly taken place that day. Larry confirmed to several friends and a few gang members the exact truth, as dad advised him to.

Again, as dad explained to Larry, "I said my piece, and still was allowed to walk out. This means that Paolo and his boys either believe maybe I could stalk them down or maybe our standing up to them gained us their respect. They don't know it, but I'm going to pick my spot to even the score. My words are imprinted in their minds. I got them thinking."

Fast forward two months and the minor incident was blown greatly out of proportion. By the last report, the story on the street was that Paolo had Dad and Larry almost on their knees begging not to beat them and both apologized over and over for the threat Dad had made. Paolo felt sorry for them and let them pass.

It was time once again for the annual shop picnic. Everyone began talking about those whose kid would win the contests, and if Joe from the tool crib would sing Italian songs with his accordion again this year.

As Saturday approached, word on the assembly line had it that four or five people were advised to stay home by the shop gang members. Two of the five were Dad and Larry. They were being accused of promoting a hostile lack of respect toward the gang. Dad heard about the rumor and laughed out loud to be sure he was heard.

For a full week the main conversation up and down the several production lines was about the upcoming picnic. The gang leaders were pleased with the rank and file since landing roles in the local shop bargaining team. Paolo's boys won by a large majority. Paolo claimed it was an honest and open election, and he commented that he would have a recount if anyone cared to make such a motion. As no hands were raised at Paolo's offer, the vote carried. Paolo added, "Because of the strong support our team received, we will donate and roast a pig for the picnic to show our appreciation."

It was clear to Dad and Larry that their days of working in an atmosphere of intimidation and fear would not be coming to an end soon. They both agreed that if offered a retirement package, they would take it. However, in the meantime, they were excited about the upcoming festivities.

Around sunrise that Saturday, Paolo's boys opened the park and bean the long slow roasting of a pig, stocked the bar with plenty of soft drinks and liquor.

At noon the gates officially opened and in rolled bicycles, several motorcycles, and cars full of employees and management. Management had hired a small band named Stanley and the True Tones. Dad remembered the group from a family wedding the prior summer. The softball, horseshoes, and badminton equipment were set up and ready to go.

Even Father Sullivan showed up to be sure everyone would behave. He always reserved the table about 10 feet from the bar so he could make sure nobody overindulged, as had been the case in past years. Father Sullivan was a very well-respected priest. As he confessed, "I do take a sip of the devil's broth on special occasions for my nagging arthritis." Over the years, people laughed with Father Sullivan, cried with him, prayed with him, but mostly loved him.

Wallace Park was a big park. It spread out from the pavilion across the softball field, a horseshoe area, two tennis courts, two basketball courts, and an area for badminton. There was plenty of room for all the employees to spread out and fully enjoy the afternoon.

Father Sullivan managed to get everyone together for an opening prayer, and Tool Crib Joe played the Star-Spangled Banner on his accordion. It was officially party time!

Several volunteers cooked hot dogs and burgers, while Paolo's boys watched over the roasting pig, and served up salads, chips, and other sides. Their efforts were much appreciated by those who simply kicked back to enjoy themselves.

The bar was opened, and the band began to play. Tool Crib Joe warmed up for a song or two after a few relaxing beers.

Because of the acreage of the park, and the spread-out activities of the employees, Paolo and Dad did not come face-to-face for most of the day. Any thoughts of another possible showdown had waned. Such a showdown would have ended very badly, so it was best avoided.

There were three or four different factions that stayed in their own groups throughout the day. Each group respectfully shared the food and open bar with all others but otherwise kept to their tight groups.

As the afternoon went along people ate and drank and played games and the food and beverage department had a constant stream of customers. During the feast, folks also learned about the traditions attached to the long and laborious job of roasting a pig.

When the clock struck 5 p.m., the crowd mellowed. Those guests with small children started packing up for home. The band took a break and many of the older folks were already headed out.

The folks all said goodbye and said their "thank yous" to the shop managers for the fun day. As the crowd thinned, the sound of people shouting rose up from the biker group. Then we heard what nobody wants to hear at a picnic that has a heavy Hispanic attendance. A loud voice yelled, "Instead of cooking a pig, they should have cooked a few of you lousy spics!"

When Dad heard this, he was well aware of what had happened to prompt the incendiary comment, and what would likely happen next. The Hispanic/Latino guests were still gathered. Several bikers who were from other towns and were just guests of employees, were doing all the shouting and name calling.

The bikers that were employees were friends with both sides. The Hispanic employees had no interest in fighting the legitimate biker employees that they worked with and had lunch with every workday in the shop lunchroom.

Now both groups were facing off. The women, children, and management left before circumstances got worse. The two sides were about even in number, but the employees headed for their cars. This caused the Hispanic group to slowly melt away rather than fight the biker thugs.

Continued swearing and open challenges from the bikers caused a hush to come over both crowds. Suddenly out of the Hispanic group stepped Paolo. He stepped out of the crowd alone and pushed his way out into the space between the two factions. He shouted to the gang leader of the bikers to step out and face him.

Now there were two groups facing each other with about 50 feet between them. In that space Paolo stood alone, telling the bikers to leave and let his people leave. The bikers laughed as the swearing and threats got louder. Paolo said he and his friends were going to walk to their cars and leave peacefully. Even more laughter followed his comment.

That's when Dad walked out of the small crowd and headed out to stand next to Paolo. Paolo was stunned to see this man who he was at odds with a few days earlier making a stand with him. Both crowds were on edge. What was the old man doing out there, another man questioned.

Dad quickly shouted to the employee bikers caught up in the biker gang, "Pepe, Jose, Papo, you know me and Paolo. Tell your friends we mean no harm to anyone. We live in the United States where we can all meet for a day of fun. We are asking you again to tell them to stand down and let us pass or you will have to kill me and that's no way to end this beautiful day!"

Paolo spoke out that in our shop there is no discrimination, that we all lived in the same neighborhood and had kids here on both sides that were watching this showdown.

"Let's show them how to be real Americans!" Dad shouted. Some of the guys on both sides clapped and then silence followed.

Larry and his wife were first to leave, and others quickly followed. Before anybody could get their cars, three squad cars wheeled in with a flurry of dust and surrounded the area.

Officer O'Neill saw the two groups and jumped in the middle of the space where Paolo and Dad stood. He shouted his question loud and clear, "George, are we about to have a problem with our biker friends?"

Dad replied, "No, no, no. After such a great picnic we were all just saying goodbye. In fact, Paolo even invited the biker guests back next year."

The biker gang made phony friendly gestures to our side, and Paolo openly expressed his appreciation for their help and repeated his thanks in Spanish to everyone's delight.

The crowd also knew that Paolo had just saved the biker boys from serious legal difficulties. The shop employee bikers saw two different sides to Paolo and Dad that day.

One side was that of two courageous men to face a motorcycle gang alone. And the other was that of genuinely good guys to not accuse the gangs of bullying or harassment.

The young officer stated he wasn't convinced that we were all wishing each other goodwill, so he stayed until the last person left the park.

Paolo shyly turned to Dad and asked, "What the hell do we do next?"

Dad replied, "Go over and thank the gang leader for not carrying this any farther, and that he didn't have to kill me and the old man."

On the way out, Paolo said thank you to Dad for his support. Dad ended the dialogue by saying, "Paolo, I have given you two free lessons on how to survive a showdown you surely would lose."

Paolo laughed. Dad winked at him and with a smirk on his face said, "Paolo, could you tune your boys down a notch in the shop?

Paolo laughed again and ended by saying, "I guess I will have to. I don't want to have to kill you."

Chapter 15

The Pie Man

It's not that it was such a bad day, it just wasn't such a good day. For three young boys living in a quiet, Connecticut farm community, even a rainy day was an event.

Friday afternoon was one of those "be grateful you live here" days. I was reminded by Mom that we should pray for all those poor children in China who didn't have enough food to eat. I had never seen a real live Chinese person, but I believed mom.

It sometimes seemed the only exciting event we could count on was waiting for the Howdy Doody show to come on TV.

My friend Allen's parents invited all the kids to come in at 4 p.m. to watch the show. The Wordens had the only TV in the neighborhood. The broadcast of Howdy Doody always followed Kate Smith singing

"God Bless America" or "When the Moon Comes Over the Mountain."

It was mid-summer and the novelty of no school and no homework was beginning to wear thin. Also, being summer, it was harvest and sale time for many local farmers.

This meant we could go visit Uncle Joe sitting at his roadside vegetable stand. He set his business up under the giant maple tree along the driveway every year. He always had a spare basket of fresh strawberries and plenty of stories he would share. We had heard them all many times but loved hearing them again and again.

On this day, Uncle Joe was upset about something and didn't have a story for us. He shared more of a complaint about how the traffic raced up and down our country road. He managed to keep us listening by telling us about all the close calls he and his vegetable stand had survived throughout the years, because of a small bump in the road.

We pulled up tomato baskets and sat down. He told us about delivery trucks, cars, motorcycles, and one farm tractor that had lost control and crashed. At that time, I was sure that there could not be a more dangerous bump along any road anywhere in the world.

The bump or small knoll in the road was typical of country roads at the time, with few roads paved like today. During the early years of paving, much of the work was done by hand with hand tools. The small rural towns could not afford paving and earth-moving equipment. The universal remedy was to just pave over it. Our knoll was not unusually dangerous unless you were speeding.

As the afternoon passed, commuter traffic picked up. The high school buses for the summer school kids ran by and bounced over the knoll. We had never noticed the vehicles bounding over the bump until Uncle Joe's crash tales.

As we sat and watched the traffic run the gauntlet past our house, we began to realize how pathetic this pastime was. Why were three young boys spending their vacation time watching traffic? Uncle Joe was right, a speeder could lose control, but it wasn't happening on our watch.

Just as we were getting ready to go frog hunting, we spotted a good-sized box truck heading for the bump much faster than any of the earlier vehicles. We got closer and thought this truck might verify all of Uncle Joe's tales.

We recognized the truck at once. It was the Frisbie Pie truck. It had the name on the truck in large red and blue lettering. The truck body was bright white with two large pies painted on each side. It was one of the company's older delivery trucks. As it approached, you could plainly see that it was a vintage vehicle. The truck did not have the modern suspension assembly that newer trucks had, and it was rocking and rattling even on the better portion of the road.

As the truck barreled past the stand, we heard Uncle Joe yell at the driver to slow down, followed by a chorus of Italian swearing. As though it was a scene from a movie, the old truck came barreling down the last 50 feet of level road approaching the bump. All eyes were on the truck as the front wheels went up the hump. It reminded me of the Great White Whale breaching in the "Moby Dick" movie. As the front slammed into the hump, we heard a loud screech. The rear doors of the old truck popped open.

As the front end met the downslope side of the hump, the rear of the truck flew upward. This seesaw effect jarred the pie racks inside the truck loose. The pies and the pie racks on one side of the truck were catapulted out of the two rear doors. Was this a dream on our part or were we really seeing the back of the Frisbie Pie truck spew pies up along our road? It was a dream come true. At least 10 to 15 pies landed outside the truck along with the broken pie racks.

As the truck finally landed on the other side of the knoll, the driver pulled off to the side of the road. He was a bit shaken but okay. The truck was also a bit shaken but okay.

Fortunately, there were no vehicles behind to receive the barrage of pies, but unfortunately, there was Uncle Joe. Yes, his stand, his dog Booty, the first two rows of tomatoes, and Uncle Joe were hit by a combination of blueberry and apple pies.

When the volley of pies hit the road and vegetable stand, several boxes broke apart on impact, spreading pie shrapnel all about.

Uncle Joe began swearing in Italian again as the driver humbly approached. As he and Uncle Joe tried to clean the pie off the tomatoes, Booty ate the apple crumb pie off his coat, like an episode from "Our Gang Comedy."

The driver tried to wipe the blueberry filling off Uncle Joe's hat and right arm, hoping to calm him down. As we five witnesses stood dumb-founded, we began to laugh as we helped clean the apple pie filling off the tomatoes.

Coincidentally, we learned that the driver was a top manager in the Frisbie production plant located in the next town up. Worse than that for him, he was also the son of the owner. He explained that he was just filling in for the regular driver and was not familiar with our bump.

The setting quickly turned into a pie picnic. We got our tomato baskets, and we all chose a pie to eat. As we sat enjoying the pie and the conversation, each of us realized that we had just experienced the story of a lifetime.

The driver paid Uncle Joe for the three baskets of apple pie—tomato mix, to compensate for damages. He was sure the people in the pie bakery would put them to good use.

As the pie man drove on, we all sat and digested the pie and the pie truck adventure.

Thanks to the Frisbie Pie truck and tomato stand mishap, it wasn't that it was such a good day that made the incident memorable—it was a great day!

About the Author

George Gdovin is the author of *Memories, Memories, and Miracles,* a revealing true story of his struggle with alcoholism and addiction. His first book, *A light Unto You,* was published under the pseudonym, Oliver N. Tredway, and is considered a favorite among many in the AA community for its encouraging message.

Gdovin is a 40-year veteran of the building trades, having served as a building official for both residential and commercial inspection.

He lives in Guilford, Connecticut with the love of his life, Janice. He is also the proud father of two grown sons.

His next book will feature highly entertaining stories of his living and working in Guilford.